LIFE TIES

CULTIVATING
RELATIONSHIPS
that make
LIFE WORTH LIVING

Judith Balswick & Boni Piper

InterVarsity Press
Downers Grove, Illinois

InterVarsity Press® is the book-publishing division of InterVarsity Christian Fellowship®, a student movement active on campus at hundreds of universities, colleges and schools of nursing in the United States of America, and a member movement of the International Fellowship of Evangelical Students. For information about local and regional activities, write Public Relations Dept., InterVarsity Christian Fellowship, 6400 Schroeder Rd., P.O. Box 7895, Madison, WI 53707-7895.

Scripture quotations, unless otherwise noted, are from the New Revised Standard Version of the Bible, copyright 1989 by the Division of Christian Education of the National Council of the Churches of Christ in the U.S.A. Used by permission. All rights reserved.

Cover illustration: Roberta Polfus

ISBN 0-8308-1614-3

Printed in the United States of America ∞

Library of Congress Cataloging-in-Publication Data

Balswick, Judith K.
   Life ties: cultivating relationships that make life worth living/
   Judith Balswick and Boni Piper.
        p.   cm.
   Includes bibliographical references.
   ISBN 0-8308-1614-3 (paper: alk. paper)
     1. Interpersonal relations—Religious aspects—Christianity.
   2. Intimacy—Religious aspects—Christianity.   3. Christian life.
   I. Piper, Boni.   II. Title.
   BV4597.52.B35   1995
   248.4—dc20   95-40448
                                                                          CIP

21	20	19	18	17	16	15	14	13	12	11	10	9	8	7	6	5	4	3	2	1
13	12	11	10	09	08	07	06	05	04	03	02	01	00	99	98	97	96	95

To Jack and Don

*and others to whom
we've become intimately tied*

Acknowledgments

When for more than twenty years you have dreamed of writing a book together, it's delightful to have an editor respond enthusiastically to the first draft. We thank Rodney Clapp for helping our dream come true. He gently guided the project from beginning to end with helpful suggestions, skillful editing and, most of all, encouraging comments.

We want to acknowledge our husbands, Jack and Don, for their confidence in us as we first considered this book. Their belief in our dream kept us believing it too. They helped us get free to vacation together in Portugal, where this book was conceived. We love them for encouraging our time together.

Our friend Kay Klein freely gave of herself and provided crucial input that greatly enriched this book. For her untiring reading of so many drafts, and for her friendship, love and encouragement, we are most grateful.

We also thank our friends Jim Klein and Richard Jones for rescuing us in our computer ignorance. And our thanks to Ruth Goring, senior copy editor, for her helpful input.

Friends, clients and family members have contributed significant pieces to our lives, our healing and the intimacies that have shaped us. We couldn't have written this book without them.

That we have grown more intimate in the writing of this book is evidence of the deepening ties that bind us together in God's love. We are thankful to God.

1

THE SECRET YEARNING

A *number of years ago I (Boni) felt everything in my life was* falling apart. Struggles and difficulties piled up, and eventually I entered into an extended period of doubt. We had recently moved to Seattle, where my husband was pastoring a church. I had undergone two major surgeries in the two preceding years, and my health was still not good. The care of our two small children exhausted me. I had been a missionary, but never a "pastor's wife" before, and was more than a little anxious about fitting into my new role.

Because of the surgeries, I was struggling with regulating my thyroid intake, and I knew I would soon need to be taking estrogen as well. Recovery was proving to be harder than the doctors had made it sound. My moods fluctuated, my energy level varied from day to day, and I felt stability slipping away from me.

Then the worst of it hit. One day I awoke with an enormous feeling of dread. Where was God anyway? Was God real? Was this whole Christian thing a figment of my imagination? My world felt gray and cloudy; I was deeply, intensely depressed.

Consumed with doubt, I didn't know where to turn. What would my husband think if I told him my feelings? What would the church members think if they knew I was questioning my beliefs? Had I made any friends who were close enough to be honest with? I was the pastor's wife—I had to be OK! But I wasn't, and I needed to talk to someone.

I pleaded with God to help me. That was a strange thing to do, because I was struggling even to believe he was there. Yet I felt I had to turn to him, just in case. I prayed, "God, if you are there, help me!" and I kept appealing to him through the long period of doubt that followed. But God seemed very silent.

Next I went to my husband. With tears and anguish I poured out my emotions. He comforted me lovingly and accepted my feelings. Later he told me how frightening the experience was for him. We were a team. Could he continue pastoring with a doubting wife? How could he help me when all I could see was despair?

Being the wise man that he is, he listened well and then helped me see the medical aspect of the problem: the lack of thyroid and estrogen was doing strange things to my emotions. My doctor took the situation seriously and began to work with me to help restore my perspective. Within days the despair was gone, but the doubts about God remained.

In church I felt like a terrible fake. There I sat with all the other believers, worshiping, praying, singing, fellowshiping, and I doubted it all! I was terrified that they would know, yet I hated feeling so alone.

After months of pain, I could stand it no longer. My isolation was killing me. I was who I was, and somebody besides my husband needed to know about it.

I began by telling a friend. Very carefully I expressed my doubts and my feelings, hoping she would be able to hear without being overwhelmed.

When I was done she offered a life-giving response: "Boni, I feel like I am standing on a rock in the middle of a raging sea. I feel solid on that rock and know exactly where I am. Right now you are in the water, but I've got you by the hand. I know you are doubting, but I'm not. I'm securely on the rock holding on to my friend."

I kept that image with me for years as I continued to struggle with doubt. My friend's acceptance and stability were a tremendous help to me.

Then I told my prayer group at church. I feared that they would respond with horror: "And you are the *pastor's wife?*" But, for the most part, they didn't. A few could not bear to believe that I really struggled, but the majority kept me in their prayers, allowed me to talk and loved me.

Being honest with God, my husband, my friends and my group led to an intimacy that brought me through the most difficult time in my life. Others believed when I couldn't. They prayed with me, listened to me, loved me and refused to give up on me.

I vividly remember when the doubts lifted. One evening as I sang praise to God with the rest of the prayer group, I suddenly realized how deeply I believed what I was singing. I cried tears of joy, knowing that my emotions were matching my mind again. I was not depending only on intellectual belief in God. My *heart* was thrilled to be praising him!

An Ache That Won't Quit

Intimacy is one of our most wonderful yet frightening experiences. Times of deep understanding between ourselves and our husbands, times of telling a trusted friend what we're thinking and feeling, times of warm connection with our children, times of revealing personal discouragement to a therapist or small group—these are what living is all about. And it scares us to death!

Intimacy. Communion. Connection. Because we are human, we long for these experiences. Yet we run from closeness in fear of truly being known.

We ache for something more in life. We wonder if this is all there is. We question whether others have found something we haven't. We frantically seek answers to our loneliness and brokenness. Would a new job do it? Or a new spouse? A new church or a new city? We yearn to feel connected, but we come up empty and don't know where to turn.

A Desire to Be Known

What exactly is it we want when we say we want to be known? Most of us want the comfort and healing that come from having someone know us deeply. We have a secret desire to be understood at the very core of our being. Yet this innermost part we so desperately want to share is also the part we go to great lengths to hide from others and ourselves. How, then, you may ask, do we ever dare take the risk of being close? How then can we ever hope to be healed? These are the very questions that inspired us to write this book. Twenty years ago Judy and I discovered the healing that can come from intimate friendship.

When Judy's husband, Jack, was awarded a Fulbright scholarship for a year in Cyprus, she felt a little fearful. She had grown up in the American Midwest and had never even traveled outside the United States. How would her seven- and eight-year-old children adjust to a different culture and school system? Away from her counseling practice and friendships, how would she spend her days?

Living in Cyprus proved fascinating—there is always so much to learn in a new culture—but, as she had feared, Judy found herself lonely after Jack and the kids left home each morning. In the solitude, feelings of vulnerability and pain rose to the surface.

Feeling helpless, she prayed, pouring out her need to God.

At that time my husband and I were serving as missionaries in Cyprus. I had been teaching Bible, but after our son was born I left the classroom and stayed at home with him. A few individuals would come to our house to study Scripture with me. That time at home gave me quietness to think through some important life issues. But, like Judy, I struggled with feeling lonely.

One evening after the English service at church we invited the Balswick family home to swap stories of traveling in the Middle East. After dinner, Judy's family left and my family went to bed. But Judy and I settled in to get to know each other better.

We sat in front of a fire, each wrapped in a blanket. And in that unheated apartment on the island of Cyprus we began to feel more warmth than we had ever experienced with a friend before. We began telling our stories, talking of past pain and future goals. We struggled to understand each other. We dared to tell all. And surrounded by God's Spirit, we learned what it was to be known intimately by another.

In the wee hours of the morning we reached out to clasp hands in a covenant of love that has undergirded our friendship through all the years since. In this treasured friendship, and in other intimate relationships, we have both found much healing and wholeness.

Thomas Oden (1974) defines intimacy as a mosaic of two persons putting together moments of personal closeness that are unique to the two of them. Although this deep sense of knowing most often happens between two people, we believe it is possible to be intimate in family relationships, groups and even communities where people are able to interact in personal and affectionate ways. Intimacy is an intensely personal relationship of sustained closeness where each knows and is known by the other.

Have you ever had the privilege of being close to another like this? It is an incredible experience to have another person know you so well. Most of us yearn for just that, though sometimes we wonder if anyone really cares so deeply.

Does Anybody Care Who I Am?

Most of us doubt that we are lovable. We question whether we will be accepted when and if we decide to reveal our inner self. We desperately want to believe that even when our darkest interior is revealed, we will still be loved and accepted by the person who witnesses the revelation. This desire to be intimately known and loved is a universal need. However, to reveal our inner self requires a vulnerability that often seems too scary. In self-protection we hold back from what we long for and keep ourselves hidden.

Intimacy is born out of trust and safety—an increasing scarcity in our world of suspicion and distrust. Possibly the only perfectly safe relationship is with Jehovah God, the One who loves us unconditionally and is solely deserving of our trust. Yet even here we run and hide, as if we weren't known already by our Creator. Nudged by the grace extended in Jesus, we are able to respond to God's personal invitation of love. And when we do, we are received "just as we are" and found fully acceptable in Christ. It's a miracle and the beginning of our healing process.

We are called to know God in a personal way, and in that knowing to be made whole. Romans 8 assures us, "There is therefore now no condemnation for those who are in Christ Jesus. . . . Neither death, nor life, nor angels, nor rulers, nor things present, nor things to come, nor powers, nor height, nor depth, nor anything else in all creation, will be able to separate us from the love of God in Christ Jesus our Lord." Precisely because we are no longer condemned and assured that we will never be separated from our God, we can freely let ourselves be known. First John 4:18 reminds us that "there is no fear in [God's] love, but perfect love casts out fear." The truth of these verses liberates us to be open to an all-knowing God.

Dare I Trust Others?

Even if we feel safe with Christ, we still may fear being intimate with each other. With one in two marriages ending in divorce today, many children experience broken trust that they carry into adulthood. Most of us, at one time or another, have gone through bitter disappointments, broken promises, emotional injury. Therefore, disclosing our innermost self becomes risky business and is increasingly difficult to do.

Our fears are understandable. Once our capacity for trust has been shattered, it's hard to open ourselves up to even more pain. So we shut down, close the door and keep ourselves hidden. We keep our secrets, deciding to live and die with them unresolved. The problem is that *we can't be healed until we externalize the internal.*

All of us carry pain. For some this pain is severe, resulting from difficult situations in the past. For others it comes from ongoing day-to-day challenges. Whatever the level of distress, it builds as we hold it inside ourselves. Whether you suffered abuse as a child or are feeling the sadness of sending your first child off to college, you will continue to need healing throughout your life. Allowing that ache to sit in isolation only leads to further agony. Sometimes bringing ourselves before God is all that is necessary to ease the pain, but most often we need a human companion to share the experience with us as well.

When the first Piper child left home for college, I thought I had prepared myself fairly well. After all, I had already been celebrating his success *and* mourning my loss for three months! But for a month after he left, I was physically sick with one thing and then another. It wasn't until I took a look at what was really going on with me that things began to get better. I gave myself some time to think of the implications that this first child's leaving home had for me. I then allowed myself time to mourn what I was calling "the beginning of the end"! I also talked with a friend who knew more about this stage of parenting than I did. It all helped. I grew through the mourning and rejoicing, partly because I had identified the real issue and worked with it.

When we can reveal ourselves to others and receive their input and responses, we will grow. When we allow our relationships to challenge and encourage us, we move toward wholeness. It has a spiral effect. The more we share and deepen our self-knowledge, the more we risk going to deeper levels of exposure with others, which results in more discovery of who we are. In knowing we will be known. For we find out about ourselves as we come to know and respond to others. Listening to another's self-revelation brings out our own thoughts, feelings and values.

There is no solution in isolation. Healing comes only when we acknowledge who we are to ourselves, to others and to God.

The Intimacy-Healing Connection
Healing requires that we wade through many levels of self-truth on our road to wholeness. This happens when we share ourselves intimately with someone we trust. Whether it be with God, my spouse, a friend, a therapist, a group member or a parishioner in my community of faith, sharing is part of the journey of healing.

We must choose to take the time to look inside ourselves and pay attention to the brokenness that's there. Only when we recognize that we're fractured will we seek healing.

Sometimes we think healing comes only in the therapy office or in the church. Certainly some experiences do require professional help for understanding and recovery. However, God uses relationships throughout our lives to bring the healing we need.

God's Way of Healing
In the book of James we are told, "Confess your sins to one another and pray for one another, so that you may be healed" (James 5:16).

This verse makes a direct connection between intimacy and healing. It shows that healing comes when we trust others enough to share the darkest parts of ourselves and are humble enough to ask for the prayers of others. God, we know, is the Author of healing. But it's real people, in the flesh, who convey God's love. Shedding our masks, revealing our pain and confessing to one another are God's ways of healing.

Do you long to know yourself at a deeper level? Do you desire relationships that will help you learn more about who you are and what you were created to be? Do you yearn for a deeper relationship with God, more intimacy in your marriage or family, more closeness in community? Do you see the healing potential from such relationships?

In this book we will consider how relationship intimacy affects your growth and healing process. We will focus on important relationships that God uses to bring about our wholeness. We will use stories from our own lives and the lives of others to show how healing has flowed out of closeness.

The more we have thought about the connection between intimacy and healing, the more excited we've become. There is tremendous power in affinity and affection! Can you really find healing there? Yes, we believe you can.

Questions for Thought

1. Make a list of the times you have experienced healing as a result of an intimate relationship. Is this a normal part of your healing journey? Why or why not?

2. What losses from your past make you wary of closeness now? In which of your relationships are you maintaining distance because of early loss?

3. What has been your experience of following the directives in James 5:16?

For Your Growth
Evaluate your present relationships. Are they as close as you would like? Do you find healing there? Are there changes you hope for? Determine to do one thing this week to move toward a closer relationship with one person.

2

INTIMACY WITH GOD

I *(Judy) remember the time I visited Israel, the land where Jesus* lived. I walked where he had walked. I visited Jerusalem, where he had wept for those who did not believe. I waded into the Jordan River and splashed in the very waters that had baptized him. It was an incredible, exhilarating time. I felt deeply in touch with God.

One evening I ventured out to a beautiful meadow to watch the sun set over Mount Hermon. My spirit was open to the Lord, and my heart leaped for joy in spontaneous worship. Acutely aware of God's presence, I sang out from the bottom of my heart, "How great thou art! How great thou art!" I prayed, I cried, I was silent before the Lord. The intimate communion brought healing to my soul.

Three years later I sat in my son's bedroom in deep grief after his untimely death at age nine. It had all happened so fast. It started with a simple complaint of leg pain, then a visit to the pediatrician, next a rushed trip to the hospital for x-rays, the discovery of a tumor, surgery the next day, a diagnosis of bone cancer, a month's treatment at an NIH research center, and finally the devastating announcement "There is nothing more we can do for your son." Those four months had rushed by. Our hope that a miracle would bring healing had been dashed. We'd had a few weeks at home together, and now my son was dead. It was finished! I was defeated and terribly lonely for him.

I retreated to Jeff's bedroom to be close to his things and to cry out to God. This day, when my whole world was crashing down on me, I felt the deep presence of my Lord. "The LORD is near to the brokenhearted," the psalmist says (Psalm 34:18). I lifted up moanings and groanings that were too deep for words. God met me in my distress and eased my pain. This intimate moment with God brought a healing peace that was far beyond my human understanding.

In such transforming moments of being known and feeling close to God, we take a step closer to wholeness. So don't you wonder why it seems to take a crisis or an extraordinary circumstance for us to become this connected with God? Perhaps it's when we're vulnerable that we reach to God for wisdom and comfort. It's during times when we feel deeply about what's happening in our lives that we approach God from our innermost being. The Holy Spirit entreats us to get beyond ourselves in order to understand who we are in God's light.

Seeking intimacy with God tends to be an exception rather than the rule of our lives. Why don't we find ways to draw upon God's presence in ordinary, everyday moments? Even when we know that God is accessible and Jesus invites us to come and eat with him (Revelation 3:20), even when we desperately want to connect, we don't always make the intimate connection. Perhaps we need to remind ourselves that God is trustworthy and desires to reveal himself to us.

The Extended Arm of God

One of the incredible teachings of Christianity is that we can know God intimately. How presumptuous, some would say; how dare we claim such a thing! Yet it's just the invitation Jehovah extends: to intimately know the God of the universe. Many of us want to seek God with our whole heart. We long to feel the presence of God in profound and concrete ways.

The Bible gives us examples of how our transcendent God breaks into human history in order to be intimately involved with us. Take the example of God and Moses. In Exodus 33 Moses asks the Lord to continue on with the children of Israel, even after they have betrayed him by turning to a false god of their own making. Moses knows that if God doesn't go with them in this journey, there is no point in going on. As he talks to the Lord about this, God says, "Yes, I will go with you!" (see vv. 12-17). This answer and promise is for us.

But Moses doesn't stop there. He is bold enough to ask for even more! What courage he has when he says, "Show me your glory" (v. 18). Here we might expect God to strike him dead for such an arrogant demand—that would be the end of Moses! But instead God shows Moses all that one can see of God and still live. Moses wanted more of God, and God met that desire.

In Psalm 42:1-2 the writer expresses a similar desire for God.

As the deer pants for streams of water,
so my soul pants for you, O God.
My soul thirsts for God, for the living God.
When can I go and meet with God? (NIV)

Have you ever panted for God like that? Many of us know what it is to pant for material things, but panting for God may seem a little silly. But let yourself picture it with all the graphic details—tongue hanging out, dripping of saliva, starry eyes and longing like nothing else matters . . . panting to be in close communion with God. Though we might not have chosen the image of panting to describe it, many of us yearn passionately for God in just this way.

The Old Testament tells us of others who were rewarded in their persistent desire to be close to God. Jacob had dramatic encounters with God through dreams. On one occasion God assures Jacob, "Know that I am with you and will keep you wherever you go, and will bring you back to this land; for I will not leave you until I have done what I have promised you" (Genesis 28:15). Jacob receives the promise and acknowledges, "Surely the LORD is in this place—and I did not know it!" (v. 16). Later Jacob has an experience in which he wrestles with God and will not let go until God blesses him (Genesis 32:22-32). His very name is changed because he struggles with God and prevails until God comes to him. Jacob's response is recorded in verse 30: "For I have seen God face to face, and yet my life is preserved." Jacob persisted in wanting to know God intimately, and God honored his efforts.

Hannah came to the Lord deeply depressed over her desire to have a son (1 Samuel 1). She pursued God with all her might; she didn't hide her emotions but wept openly and pleaded boldly. She even bargained with God, vowing to give her son up for the Lord's service. And when her prayer was answered, she responded passionately with a grateful heart: "My heart exults in the LORD. . . . There is no Holy One like the LORD, no one besides you. . . . For the LORD is a God of knowledge, and by him actions are weighed" (1 Samuel 2:1-3).

The God of creation relentlessly reaches out to the created ones. Michelangelo's magnificent Sistine Chapel painting pictures God with outstretched arm, hand fully extended toward Adam (representative of humankind), who is halfheartedly reaching back. God comes to us like that—reaching, stretching, extending with desire that we respond to the invitation of intimacy. It is a call of grace. The initiative is with God. As J. I. Packer says, "We do not make friends with God; God makes friends with us" (1993:41).

Love Reaching Out

God reaches out to us in three important relational ways.

☐ Through an everlasting covenant, God promises to love us unconditionally and faithfully.

☐ Through grace, God accepts us as we are and forgives us in Jesus Christ.

☐ Through empowerment, God offers us genuine life in his Holy Spirit.

When Jehovah God made a covenant with his people Israel, he promised that he would be their God and they would be his people. This agreement was initiated and instituted by God. Our God makes this same agreement today with his people, the church. He calls us to himself, to be in relationship with him and to know him intimately. We as God's people stand in the same place as Israel did long ago, with God covenanting to love us and be faithful to us and calling us to be his people and live in obedience to him. He calls us in grace, not demanding that we be worthy but accepting the payment of Jesus as sufficient for us. And he equips us to live by giving us his Spirit as our comforter and our guide.

Through the three Persons of the Trinity, God calls us to unfold ourselves without fear. Because we are God's children in relationship with our Creator God, there is potential for wholeness and healing. This is where our needs to be loved, to be forgiven, to be empowered and to be known are met. God draws, prompts and urges us into an intimate relationship with himself.

Have you responded to his call? Do you know you will be welcomed with open arms when you come? Do you know you do not have to be afraid? Have you heard that wholeness ultimately comes through Jesus?

God Among Us

The supreme act of love is that God gave his only begotten Son to live among us. Jesus entered our world in humility, as a tiny baby. Mary made space for Jesus when the angel Gabriel told her she was favored and would bear God's Son. She became vulnerable and received Christ: "Here am I, the servant of the Lord; let it be with me according to your word" (Luke 1:38). Her song of praise in Luke 1:46-55 expresses her intimate worship before God: "My soul magnifies the Lord, and my spirit rejoices in God my Savior. . . . For the Mighty One has done great things for me, and holy is his name" (vv. 46, 49).

Jesus lived among us to bring truth about himself. He knows us in all our ways, for he was like us and was tempted in every way that we are. The One who knew no sin became sin for us (Hebrews 4:15). In this intimate sacrifice of vulnerability Christ offers us redemption.

In his earthy interactions with people, Jesus knew how to be intimate. He did not brush off the little children who came to him; he received expressions of love from a prostitute who washed his feet with her tears and dried them with her hair; he stooped down to wash the feet of his friends and asked them to stay up with him in his darkest hour; he was pleased when Mary of Bethany sat at his feet to learn from him; he had compassion for those who were hungry and diseased; he wept over a friend's death; he touched the untouchables of his world; he persisted in asking his friend Peter if he loved him; he healed and restored those who were disenfranchised. Jesus tells us to follow his example.

Hide and Seek

Can you imagine seeing Jesus far off in the distance and coming toward you? You anticipate his approach with fear and trembling. As he comes closer, he looks you directly in the eyes. You lower your glance. Then he reaches out tenderly to touch your face. How do you respond? Do you receive his touch? Can you gather up the courage to touch him back? Or do you turn away and hide?

Why is it so difficult? we ask ourselves. Why would we foolishly hide from our Healer? We were created to be intimately involved with the God of our Creation, yet as part of Adam's race we resist. Our rebellion makes surrendering to God a formidable internal battle. Surrender means we must give ourselves over to God when we want to stay in charge of our own lives. We foolishly think that we can determine better than God how to run our lives. So when Christ comes, we turn away and hide. But where can we go to hide from God?

Where can I go from your spirit?
   Or where can I flee from your presence?
If I ascend to heaven, you are there;
   if I make my bed in Sheol, you are there.
If I take the wings of the morning
   and settle at the farthest limits of the sea,
even there your hand shall lead me,
   and your right hand shall hold me fast.
If I say, "Surely the darkness shall cover me,
   and the light around me become night,"
even the darkness is not dark to you;
   the night is as bright as the day,
   for darkness is as light to you. (Psalm 139:7-12)

This psalm can be both a comfort and a distress to us. When we are longing for intimacy with Christ, it is such a comfort to know we are known. It is a comfort to know that God is everywhere. There is no place we can go, to the heavens or to the depths, and not be accompanied by God.

But when things are strained between God and us, this is not comforting at all. It's distressing to know he is everywhere and we can't get away from him! He knows everything too. Before God we have no secrets, whether we want them or not.

He already knows all there is to know about us. He knows our joys and our pains, our strengths and weaknesses. He knows where there has been growth in our lives and where healing is needed. And when God, in intimate, all-knowing ways, draws close to these areas of hurt, things change. Touched with the light of God's Spirit, we are made whole. We are healed.

We Need the Lord

Do you want to be close to God? Do you recognize your heart's hunger or restlessness for God? We are a thirsty people, and Jesus calls us to come and drink. In that drinking, we find that our needs can be met by God.

But even if you yearn for God and believe he can meet your needs, you probably struggle, as we do, with how to go deeper and stay passionate in your pursuit of God. Here's where we get stuck! Personal baggage gets in the way of our becoming intimate with God. In fact some of our baggage is deliberately constructed to keep God at a distance. Our defenses solidly in place, we build walls of caution and fear.

Wall Builders

Let's look at some of the common barriers that prevent intimacy in our relationship with God.

1. Doubts and questions. There are different kinds of doubts and questions. Many are genuine and actually help us grow closer to God. In asking these questions and honestly expressing these doubts we come to understand God more fully. But at other times our inquiries and misgivings are protective screens erected to keep God at a distance.

Genuine questions and real doubts should always be addressed, but we need to rid ourselves of those doubts and questions that prevent intimacy with God. One way to find out which kind you're struggling with is to ask whether you really want an answer. Hon-

estly discerning whether the question diverts you from a relationship with God or helps you to know God better will give you a chance
to break down the barrier.

These questions take many forms. Questioning what God is doing
in family situations or in world events can make us feel helpless and
make God seem unapproachable or detached. Looking at age-old
theological debates without finding a clear answer can be frustrat-
ing. But we will be missing an opportunity for growth if we use these
questions to prevent closeness with God rather than to delve more
deeply into the mystery of God's identity.

A couple of years ago I (Boni) noticed that one of my clients, Peter,
was repeatedly raising many unresolved questions. He had become
distressed over the direction of a church ministry in which he had been
heavily involved. For years the church had supported a street ministry,
but recently had decreased its financial support in order to refurbish
the church building. How could God possibly direct that way? Peter
asked. How could God allow godly people to make those choices? How
could God allow ungodly leaders to run a godly church? He struggled
through Scripture, asking God to show him a way to confront the
materialism he saw in his church. But others did not view the situation
as Peter did, and he continued to be overwhelmed by doubts of others
and of God. He had not stopped asking questions long enough to hear
his church leaders' reasoning and to seek God's will. He came to realize
that he did not really want an answer.

The real problem was the bitterness Peter felt toward God and his
church for not being elected to a leadership position in the congregation. Part of him did not want to let go of these bitter feelings. He
was in conflict with God's will and refused to submit to it. He was
deliberately using anger, questions and doubts as a barrier to halt
closeness with God. His questions helped him keep a "safe" distance.

2. Self-imposed judgments because of sin or failure. These can
take many forms. True guilt that comes from unconfessed sin is a

barrier. When we refuse to talk to God about our sin, we widen the gap between God and us. As we hide from God, our secret creates separation. God is available to hear and forgive. But the longer we hide, the more isolation takes control of us. Being in touch with God begins to seem impossible.

Another form of self-imposed judgment is shame. Shame is different from guilt (something we *did*) in that it causes us to feel bad about ourselves (something we *are*). When we feel we are not good enough to approach God, we stay away. We assume God never would listen to someone like us. The "shame on me!" message is a broken record, repeating over and over that we are unworthy to be in God's presence. The wall of shame we erect keeps us from the God of grace who accepts us as we are.

3. Wrong beliefs about God. When our picture of God is foreboding, condemning and abusive, we do not dare approach the throne of grace. We tend to fashion God out of our experiences with authority figures. If we had unapproachable parents or teachers, knowing God as *Abba*—Daddy—is especially difficult. It is hard for us to see God as One who loves us and wants to bless us.

On the other hand, if we view God as powerless or neglectful, we find it hard to believe that he will be able to meet our needs or intervene in our lives. C. S. Lewis wrote, "May it be the real I who speaks, may it be the real Thou I speak to" (1963:82). Our false beliefs about God are barricades that keep us from the true God.

4. Fear of what we might learn if we were close to God. This can take several forms. We may not want to hear what God is asking us to do. The call may be to forgive another, to act for God in some way or to give up something in our lives. Hiding and pretending not to hear is a technique many of us learned as children. We became "deaf" so we wouldn't have to obey our parents. We think the same ploy might work with God: *If I do not know, God cannot hold me accountable.*

Sometimes we fear learning more about ourselves: *What I don't know about myself can't hurt me,* or *I know enough about me to keep me going.* God might call us to change our views, so we think it's safer not to get close enough to hear him. Our fear of knowing is often our greatest barrier to intimacy with God.

5. Anger at God. Perhaps God has not answered prayer as we wanted, or the circumstances in our lives are not to our liking. We are angry and blame God.

A few years ago Philip's wife died after a long and painful battle with cancer. Philip never has been able to deal with his belief that God put his wife through misery and then let her die. He is angry with God and no longer wants a relationship with him. "He did what he wanted to do, now I'm doing what I want," Philip says. In his anger and hurt he has withdrawn from God. The barrier has been erected because Philip wants it that way. He is keeping his main source of comfort at a distance.

6. Distracting ups and downs. We can be on top of the mountain one day and in the depths of the valley the next. Some of us allow our emotions to determine whether we are connected or disconnected to God. If we don't have good feelings at the moment, we stay away. Even though God is always available, our rhythms of receiving him are erratic and sporadic.

When life is going well, we throw God a prayer here and there, but mostly we maintain control and leave God in the background. In a crisis we do not have time for God. We allow circumstances to determine how much energy we will put into our relationship with God. If we are not experiencing closeness with God, we make no attempt at intimacy. This is more than a pulse in a normal ebb and flow of relationships. It is a polarized reaction.

Shattering the Walls
How do we go about breaking these barriers in order to seek the

Lord? Jerry Sittser gives insight in *The Adventure.* He encourages us to nurture intimacy with God in three ways—solitude, worship and sacraments. Common sense dictates that intimacy requires spending time to become acquainted, learning to listen and having opportunity to commune. This is what solitude, worship and the sacraments are all about. In solitude we listen for God's voice; in worship we express our love and longings; and in receiving the sacraments we touch and taste God's grace and presence. These actions can break the barriers and open us up to God.

This time spent with our God must be private as well as public. As Pamela Heim states in *Nurturing Intimacy with God,* "In our ignorance and distrust we've become unenthusiastic, apathetic, or unfaithful lovers of Jesus Christ" (1990:35). In human relationships where private time is unavailable, there is a limited capacity for intimacy. We do not allow ourselves to be known fully in a crowd. So it is with God. Our private time, not public appearances, is the basis for our relationship. Here our soul is open to God alone. During these moments we allow God to speak to us intimately.

To know God intimately is to know him in truth. "Most of our unfaithfulness . . . is because we've never gotten to know him well enough to realize just how splendid he is" (Heim 1990:35). To be cradled in love by the One who created, redeemed and empowered us is an awesome experience. It helps us know who we are and whose we are. Nestling us under his wings like a mother hen, God keeps us close to his heart. "The Spirit himself testifies with our spirit that we are God's children" (Romans 8:16 NIV). *Abba,* our Daddy, wants to be involved as a loving parent, the One who lifts us up, takes our hand and leads us on our journey.

Finally, just as our disobedience erected the barriers, our obedience breaks them down. The incongruity of living in disobedience—being one person on the outside and another on the inside—tears us apart. But when we trust God and obey him, we are one, whole.

We can face God confidently. We are available for intimate contact. We are ready for his healing touch.

We are open and ready for God to bring us to wholeness when we do not hide, when we understand God for who he is, when we meet privately and publicly with our Lord and when we live in obedience.

The Healing Effects

Did Jesus ever touch anything that did not benefit? We cry out to God, "We are the clay, you are the potter" (Isaiah 64:8). But when we make such a declaration we also must trust the Holy Spirit to mold us into the beautiful treasure God promises to make of us. What an intimate act—exposing ourselves in humility and submitting to God's Spirit. The only possible result is healing. God's healing power is available through Jesus, the wounded healer who knows all about our woundedness and can make us well. But we must determine to approach him for healing.

Let's strive to be honest and open with the One who is familiar with us and who knows the deepest secrets and longings of our hearts. The all-knowing Creator understands more about us than we can ever know about ourselves. And this God of all wisdom desires to be intimately involved with us on our road to wholeness.

Talk Is Not Enough

A sad realization came to us as we wrote this book. We wanted to give an example of someone we know to be truly passionate for Christ. We wanted to tell of a time when passion for Christ caused one of us to seek him with all our being. We came up blank—not because we lack desire, but somehow we do not pursue God with that kind of energy.

We do know a young man who often tells us how important Jesus is to him. He says his relationship with Christ is passionate—that he doesn't know anybody, not even at church, who is closer to God than he is. He wishes others were more like him. He is a disciplined man, choosing only to read Christian literature, never visiting a movie theater, watching a television program or engaging in chit-chat. Yet he rarely smiles, welcomes visitors at church or helps anyone. We are skeptical of his claim of intimacy with Jesus.

We have come to understand that the mark of people truly passionate about Christ is that they do not talk about it—they just do it. Outwardly they are quiet, but inwardly they have zeal to spend time with God. Such passion is noticeable only in subtle ways, because the person is not bragging about being close to God. His or her love for the Lord is expressed in consistent integrity and love.

If we are intimately related to Christ it certainly will be evident by our speech. All of our being will exude Christ's presence. No task that Jesus asks will be too small or too great. The whole purpose of living will be to honor Christ—even if others do not see what we do. Going on record as having the most intimate relationship with Jesus is not the goal. Knowing Jesus himself and striving to reveal ourselves to him is what we seek—regardless of whether that results in human admiration. We should not pursue an attitude of "Look at me!" but a lifestyle that says, "Look at Jesus!" Being spiritually fulfilled is not a position of religious arrogance. It is a life of talk, action, emotions and thought that points to our Lord.

Young people see this in adults. How uncanny it is to overhear kids talking and realize how clearly they can cut to the heart of a matter! Once I (Boni) taught a high-school class in which the lesson involved loving one another. One of the children sarcastically responded, "Oh, you mean like Mrs. Brown and Mrs. Smith?" I had assumed the young people were oblivious to the fact that these two women feuded and refused to be reconciled. Actually they all knew of this private problem, because they easily recognized phoniness.

You cannot replace true pursuit of spiritual fulfillment with superficial spiritual arrogance. We only fool ourselves. Those around us usually perceive the truth.

We are fulfilled spiritually in Christ. All that we need to be complete we already have in the Lord. But because we are thirsty, earthbound people, we need more of God. In heaven we will know God in the most intimate, personal way. Now we have a foretaste, later the full course. Wanting more of God is a sign of faith. Let's pray that the Holy Spirit stirs us to crave our Lord just as the psalmist panted for him. Such longing leads to wholeness.

The Lap of Jesus

Laying ourselves bare before God is an intimate experience. It opens us to change. As we confess to our heavenly Parent, God meets us where we are. Can you picture yourself as one of the children who boldly approached the disciples to see Jesus? Have you ever been open enough to sit on his lap, let him stroke your hair and whisper words of love in your ear? Healing comes from such familiarity with God.

Put yourself in the stories of the Gospels. Imagine being in a crowd as Jesus approaches. Sense the heat of the day, the dust in the air, the beating of your heart as you risk reaching out to touch the robe of Christ in hope of healing. Imagine climbing a tree to catch a better glimpse of him. Envision his gaze as he spots you, orders you down and invites himself to your home. Picture in your mind Jesus looking deeply into your eyes and giving the command that he also gave to his disciples: "Follow me." Visually making Scripture real increases the connection we feel with Jesus.

Have you ever imagined God's Spirit at your birth, or even before? Can you see the Spirit of love forming you, breathing life into you at birth, counting your toes and fingers and planning your future? A God of such initial involvement knows you well. The investment of such a God in your life is great. As you grow, change and struggle, that same Creator God is available for continued intimacy. And as you risk that continued intimacy moment after moment, healing can occur. You cannot be in the presence of God without profiting.

Pass It On

What does an intimate relationship with God have to do with intimate relationships with other human beings? The relationship we experience with God enables us to give unconditional love, to extend forgiveness and grace and, through the Holy Spirit, to empower others. When we experience God's faithful, unconditional love, we have a capacity to offer it to others. When we receive grace and know we are accepted, we are free to recognize and value the uniqueness of others. When we are forgiven and restored after personal failure, we will be enabled to forgive those who disappoint us. When we have been emboldened by God, we grow in our ability to share that power. And all of this leads to intimacy.

Shannon did not realize she had an addiction to prescription drugs until she opened herself to the Holy Spirit. She had rationalized her growing dependence as a way of stabilizing her behavior. But as her intimacy with Christ increased, her ability for self-deception decreased. As she admitted her problem to God, Shannon felt a weight lift and peace fall.

As her openness with Christ continued, Shannon confessed her dependency to her family and enlisted their support. Such vulnerability had been unknown in Shannon's family before. In turn, her teenage daughters began to share their true feelings.

Perhaps you have experienced forgiveness from Christ for some awful past sin only to find yourself needing to forgive another who has wronged you. The strength to forgive is drawn from the knowledge and experience of being forgiven. When we sense God's unconditional love, we can love others in the midst of their unlovely behavior.

Our personal knowledge of Christ and his Spirit increases our ability to relate to others as Jesus relates to us.

Does Intimacy Ever End?

Once we have found intimacy with God we want to keep it, even beyond our earthly life. There is an ending to the intimacy on this planet, because we are finite beings. But eternal intimacy with God never dies. The resurrection of Jesus proclaims that there is life beyond death for all who believe. We will forever be in the presence of our Creator. It is a meeting of our spirit, our true self, with the one true God. Only when we see God face to face will we truly be completely known and whole.

Our life on earth is but a glimpse of the intimacy we will have with Christ in glory. While difficult to comprehend, it is a thrilling concept. We will stand before the throne! What an awful, awesome thought had Jesus not been our righteousness. We stand without guilt because our sins that had been red as scarlet have become as white as snow (Isaiah 1:18). Now we can behold God's glory without shame and condemnation. The price has been paid and we stand before God without fear. God's covenant love, Christ's redemptive act of grace and the transforming power of the Holy Spirit bring us to complete and perfect wholeness in an intimate relationship with our Creator God.

How wonderful to know our relationship with Jesus will endure forever! The comfort and safety of God's eternity overwhelm us. Under this promise and provision we can wake up every morning, parent our children, love our spouses, interact with friends, work during the day and sleep safely at night. We are permitted to live in the shadow of God's wings as he daily breathes life into us and says "Know me."

Questions for Thought

1. God shows himself to be a relational God in several Bible passages

we have listed. Can you find other examples of this in Scripture?

2. What is your personal experience of God's relating to you through covenant, grace and empowering?

3. What barriers do you use to keep God at a distance? What suggestions do you have for clearing the way for more intimacy with God?

4. Give examples of how closeness with God has been a healing force in your life.

For Your Growth

□ Set aside a quiet time of solitude to do the meditations described in the "Lap of Jesus" section found earlier in this chapter. If you need help, try using the meditation section below.

□ Set aside a regular time to commune with your Lord. Practice listening to God. Let him speak to you in this quiet, sacred place.

Meditation

Find a place where you can sit comfortably and where you will not be interrupted for at least half an hour. Sit with your feet on the floor, your back up against the chair, your eyes closed, and concentrate on your breathing. As you exhale, allow the tension to leave your body. Breathing deeply, exhale tension, allowing yourself to relax with each breath.

Now begin to imagine the climate and scenery of Israel. It's a warm summer day; the sun shines brightly overhead. You feel the sweat of your body, the hot sun burning on your skin, the moisture on your forehead. The brightness of the day is overwhelming.

An enormous crowd gathers. Thousands have come to see Jesus, and there you are among them. You see Jesus ahead, with many people seeking his attention. You watch from a distance, hoping he will catch your eye, yet afraid that he will indeed see you. You are a child standing with other children, all hoping for a glimpse of the man you have heard so much about.

Take a step closer. Can you get a glimpse of him among the grown-ups who are trying to get a word with him? Just a step closer so you can get a better look.

There he is, just a few steps from you, and he is looking your way. His eyes meet yours as you look up. He holds your gaze; your eyes are locked in his. Looking at you all the time, he says something to one of his disciples, inviting you and the other children to come closer.

Embarrassed, you slowly walk forward, coming closer and closer to his outstretched arms. At last, reaching down, he lifts you up onto his lap. He holds you gently, yet you feel his strong arms surrounding you. You feel his breath on the back of your neck as he whispers words of love in your ear. He looks deeply into your eyes and calls you by name. Lovingly he strokes your head, holds you close and lets you know you belong to him.

Take as long as you need to maintain this image. Paint the picture clearly in your mind, to come back to again and again. Allow yourself to be held, loved, cradled by the God of the universe.

3

INTIMACY WITH SELF

At *age thirty-five, it seemed a little late for me (Boni) to be* asking the "who am I?" question. Yet that is what I did, and it was frightening. Of course I had asked the question before and would ask the question again. But at that point in my life, the answer had never seemed so important, so threatening or so far beyond my reach. Remembering that God already knew the answer made the question a little less frightening. My Creator God knows who I am.

We often identify our existence in terms of someone else's being. I have been identified in many ways: as the pastor's wife, Sarah's mom, Don's spouse, Christie's teacher, Bill's therapist, Judy's friend. But rarely am I seen gaining my identity from my status as God's child. Jesus Christ is the source of who we are, so to know ourselves, we need to be intimate with the One who knows us in every way.

Being aware of yourself in Christ is your primary source of

knowing. Another source is knowing yourself through the significant people in your life. Ask yourself, *What are my important relationships, and what do these people mean to me?* These are the people who are in your current healing journey.

A deeper knowing comes when you explore past relationships. Examining past relationships with parents and siblings leads to a better understanding of who you are today. Understanding your life as a little child and through later stages enables you to understand present reactions and fears. This knowledge also helps you accept victories, failures, strengths and weaknesses in a useful way.

A certain amount of self-knowledge is necessary to accept and use the gifts we have received. An ability to know who we are and what we are capable of—and then bless each other with the gifts God gives—can ease the community's burden and be helpful to everyone involved.

This chapter will focus on different aspects of knowing yourself— as a child of God, as a relational being, as many different parts and as uniquely gifted. These pieces are needed to finish the puzzle of who you are. We are convinced that self-intimacy brings healing and is a worthy process.

Know Whose You Are

The psalmist marvels that even before we are formed in the womb, God knows us. As we saw in the previous chapter, our Creator reaches to the utter depth of our being in his desire to know us:

O LORD, you have searched me
    and you know me.
You know when I sit and when I rise;
    you perceive my thoughts from afar. . . .
    You are familiar with all my ways.
Before a word is on my tongue
    you know it completely, O LORD. . . .

For you created my inmost being;
  you knit me together in my mother's womb.
I praise you because I am fearfully and wonderfully made.
  (Psalm 139:1-4, 13-14 NIV)

This is a picture of one known deeply. God is portrayed as the Creator who has intimate and infinite knowledge of us. He can be trusted to establish our identity.

Knowledge about ourselves comes by searching the Scriptures. As we read through the Bible, we view a picture of God as well as a picture of ourselves. We are amazed to learn that we are made in the image of God, and confronted by the realization that we are a fallen image. Our humanness is declared and we see our need for God and the transformation that comes through the Holy Spirit.

Look and See

David, one whose sin is recorded in Scripture, boldly asked God to examine him: "Search me, O God, and know my heart; test me and know my anxious thoughts. See if there is any offensive way in me, and lead me in the way everlasting" (Psalm 139:23-24 NIV).

Perhaps David really wanted to be known intimately by God so that he could know himself. He must have had a secure relationship with God to ask such a question. We know David sinned, yet his faith in God's grace surpassed self-criticism. Submission is an agonizing confession that brings us into an intimate knowing before God.

Are you willing to meet God at this level to know who you are? Our only hope of true self-awareness lies in coming into the presence of God to listen to his voice. In silence we wait to hear about ourselves as God defines us. And by his Spirit we dare to ask what God expects.

God wants each of us to deal with our fallenness. We are tempted to be more concerned with the areas that need changing in the lives of those around us. However, our assignment is to work on our own growth, with the help of God's Spirit.

Tell Me Who I Am, Lord

Jesus alone can reveal who we are. Our identity is in him because he lived as a human in all the ways we do. We have a tendency to rely on messages from others in determining who we are. Often we define ourselves by what others tell us or by what we hear in the media. Yet any definition of us apart from God's definition only gives a false impression.

The first aspect of intimacy with self is to move beyond our limited thinking and to hear what God wants to reveal. In quiet submission before our Creator we ask about the meaning of our existence. We come before God acknowledging that we are his creation and that we are dependent on him. Scripture teaches that we are made in God's image, that we have sinned and need a redeemer, that God loves us and has provided the redeemer, that we have been adopted as children of God and that we have a purpose as we live and work in the created world.

Listening to God's Spirit must be a regular part of prayer time. Keep a journal of all that God says to you, and see how it lines up with Scripture. We need God's guidance and renewal as we enter into the intimate place with our heavenly Parent, who is always there with arms open, ready to teach. The Holy Spirit reveals God's truths and empowers us to move in the direction of wholeness.

Knowing Yourself in Relationship

Those committed to our growth will support and encourage us in our process of knowing who we are and whose we are. The Holy Spirit transforms us, but God uses others to work his purposes also.

Intimacy with self is possible when we become acquainted with the inmost character of our own selves. Finding those fundamental, essential and private elements gives us a greater ability to lead our lives in a balanced and fruitful way.

Renowned psychologist Erik Erikson described intimacy as having a capacity for mutuality. He suggested that people must establish an identity of their own before they can be intimate. Social scientists tell us that the development of self comes when we see ourselves the way others see us. This self is reflected as others mirror us back in their definitions of who we are. By accepting this definition of self, we accumulate certain roles which are integrated into that definition. We develop values, personal preferences, limitations, likes and dislikes through our interactions with others.

The Distorted Mirror

We all know people who have fallen into the perfectionism trap. Sometimes we are so fearful of people discovering who we really are that we put on a show of goodness. Before long we begin to believe the distorted picture ourselves. As judgmental people, we often hide behind a wall built for our own security. And then from that safe place we project our sin onto those around us. Hiding sin in our own lives that we refuse to tolerate in others takes little effort. Those who tend to gossip often are the first to criticize others for spreading rumors. Those who have been confronted about their own lustful desires are quick to point out similar problems of those they know. When we do confront sin in our lives, we expect the whole world to shape up and immediately do likewise.

As we age, this pattern is more apparent. Judging others for faults we wrestle with is common behavior. This becomes a familiar trap for those who struggle with a negative self-image.

In my younger days, I (Boni) tended to believe that any criticism of me had to be valid. Having a negative view of myself, I assumed what others saw and said about me was more accurate than what *I* thought or felt. I have changed. Now when I hear criticism—of a group, someone else or me—I ask a few questions to check the credibility of the message. If it does not ring true, I begin to wonder about the sender. What is she trying to communicate? Why is the report necessary? What in his own life does he need to examine to move beyond this?

Projection is a psychological term referring to the tendency to place one's own feelings, actions or thoughts on another. We see projection with couples in therapy. A wife who is having an affair becomes overly critical of her husband for not accounting for his whereabouts. He comes home late from work, and she begins to accuse him of disloyalty, disregarding her own actual infidelity. She has projected her actions onto him.

We project with each other when we are overly critical of people struggling with the same sin we are fighting. Most of us realize how poorly we measure up when we check the standard God has set in Scripture. Who can fully obey the Ten Commandments or follow the standards in the epistles without faltering? We may avoid the big-ticket sins—adultery, stealing and murder—but who among us has not coveted? How often have we turned our back on the needs of a fellow believer or dismissed Jesus' teaching to turn the other cheek? Paul's lesson of love in 1 Corinthians 13 is a standard we all fail to attain.

In light of God's Word and his infinite grace, we have difficulty knowing how to view ourselves. The human reaction often is to become a perfectionist or to give up entirely. When we cannot perform flawlessly, we may respond by quitting or by judging others.

Whom Do You See?

Usually we learn to play a specific role in relationships. Recently I (Boni) led a group therapy session where I asked members to simply draw a picture without talking. Giving no other instructions, I left the room, letting them determine how to proceed with the exercise.

I had set up a dilemma for group members, who had to figure out how to interact to accomplish the task.

After completing the drawing, group members discussed what happened. We learned that one member, a take-charge person, began drawing immediately. Another member began drawing her own picture, completely separate from the illustration already started, on the corner of the page closest to her. Uncomfortable with the assignment, she drew her favorite escape scene, a private beach where she could be alone with her anxiety. In the exercise she withdrew, as she does in life. A third member tried to link the two pictures already begun. As she often does with her family, she strived to make her contribution accommodate the efforts of others. In this simple drawing exercise, group members reenacted their typical ways of relating to life. This experience gave them insight into how they functioned in relationship to others, improving their opportunity to change.

The Unique Me

Acceptance of self occurs when we see our image reflected in thoughts, feelings and behaviors. We see that we are different from others, which is not always a comfortable experience. It takes courage and a fair amount of security to allow ourselves to be distinct. And in the process of becoming a separate self, we may be fearful that we will lose our identity. Yet when we reveal our true self, rather than one others expect us to be, our self-definition is established.

You cannot be intimate until you confront yourself. Examine your current and past relationships. Is who you are in the presence of others who you want to be? What keeps you in that position? How can you break free of behavior that is incongruent with the self you want to be?

When you can honestly inspect your interactions with others and become aware of your own needs, expectations, disappointments and hurts, you may be able to take the beginning step in learning to accept yourself. On a piece of paper, write down the names of the significant persons in your life. Next, make four columns indicating needs, expectations, disappointments and joys. Take time to note the thoughts and feelings that come to you about these people. Seeing things written down often helps to clarify vague perceptions. A trusted friend may be willing to listen and help you decipher realistic and unrealistic responses. This recording and processing helps you know yourself better and can lead to changing behavior in order to change relationships. It gives you new choices with potential for growth and health.

In later chapters we will discuss how specific relationships can further growth. As you know yourself better through being intimately involved with others, you open yourself to greater possibilities of healing.

Knowing Your Different Parts

Have you wondered how you can function so well at work but seem so inept elsewhere? Have you questioned why you can be so together in one activity, then plummet to the depths moments later? Have you been surprised by how mature you are in most interactions, but find yourself acting like a four-year-old child in a doctor's office? Have you wondered how you could be the life of the party one evening, then sulk in the corner by yourself the next time? Occasionally we chalk it up to our moods; sometimes we worry that there is something really wrong with us. But often it is merely the various parts of our personality on parade. Let me (Judy) illustrate by sharing some of my inner parts.

When I am teaching, writing and supervising students, the "Judith K." side of me performs best. "Suzy Q," the part of me who is spontaneous, fun-loving and spacy, would never make it through a lecture. My students may enjoy this part of my personality at a party or even appreciate my humor in the classroom, but they would never learn much from Suzy Q. My "Jude" part is the compassionate counselor who is extremely sensitive to client needs. She draws on the knowledge Judith K. learns from family therapy books. In fact, these two make a nice combination until my harsh manager, "Edith," comes into the picture. She is good at bossing, controlling, judging and alienating. Edith is better kept in the background, but she often emerges when it is time to grade exams. She can be too critical and needs to be tempered by Jude. My wounded child is "Bethy." She can barely talk and aches to be comforted. Bethy would not do well in the classroom or at a party, but she helps me understand the desperate pain that my clients share.

As you can observe, naming my parts has helped me recognize their impact on my everyday life. Knowing that these segments exist as components of my personality frees me to be who I need to be in various situations. I, Judy, am definitely in charge and take leadership. When making decisions, I am aware of the different perspectives and listen to the inner voices of each character. There is an appreciation for the parts that constitute the whole of who I am.

The central me, the self, organizes the inner parts. By being in touch with all parts I will not be tempted to deny any component of myself. Neither will I give any one part more power than is needed. I can be harmonious with myself through the knowledge of my many selves.

When we are in a vulnerable place these internal parts may become more extreme, making it harder to maintain balance and leadership. For example, last spring our son Joel had been scheduled for surgery to correct a chronic liver disease he has had for more than ten years. As you would expect, I felt anxious on the morning of the surgery. After we checked Joel into the hospital, our surgeon suggested that we go about our normal daily tasks and not return for at least six hours. Can you imagine the stirring going on inside me that day? My frightened little girl part quaked, while my manager part told me to be tough and strong. Judith K. decided to teach her morning class, but the remaining parts panicked at such a notion. The multiple voices generally can be tempered in normal situations, but in a crisis mode they pulled at me in dramatic ways.

I decided to be as honest and congruent as I could with my class. I shared my fearful parts with my students, and they gladly offered prayers of love for my family and me. Being vulnerable helped them connect with me intimately. I felt good not having to fake strength or to hide fear. I then could shift gears and let Judith K. teach. My lecture may have been a bit shaky, but I lasted through the two-hour class with the support of my students. Later, in the hospital waiting room, close friends surrounded me when our surgeon announced, "I believe your son is cured!" We celebrated the good news with prayers of thanksgiving.

The Exiled Parts
Recently the concept that we have many selves within has gained attention. Family therapist Richard Schwartz describes this internal component in terms of three main categories: exiles, managers and firefighters. These internal selves seem to take on a life of their own as they try to protect and help us, even though they sometimes act in self-defeating ways. By identifying these different components of ourselves, we understand our conflicting reactions to events.

Each of us carries around the life of our childhood, with the joys, blessings, hurts and fears that came with it. The child continues to have a voice in us, for out of those memories and experiences our adult selves are formed.

For some, the child thrived and continues to flourish in the adult. If childhood was a safe place of comfort and love where adults exhibited trust and reliability, children gained confidence in their world. As adults they feel at one with their childhood being. The child of their past continues to live in healthy memories and has been incorporated harmoniously in adult years. This childhood part expressed through the adult is spontaneous, playful, delightful and engaging.

But for some, childhood was terrifying. No trustworthy adults were present. Feelings and tears were not permitted. These children survived on their own with no one to take proper care of them. They became their own caretakers in order to endure. To cope, these damaged parts disappeared into exile deep down inside. These parts may revive themselves in adulthood through fearful, skeptical, anxious, constrained or angry behavior.

Most of us fall between these two extremes, experiencing both good and bad memories. Hank had fond recollections of his family. His home had been a secure place where he felt loved. However, elementary school had terrorized him. Day after day he had been tormented on the playground, and no adults had brought an end to the suffering. Consequently he became fearful of peers and preferred being alone as much as possible. While some of his memories were warm and wonderful, others produced nightmares. His damaged inner child made him wary and defensive as an adult around his friends. This skeptical child part interfered with his ability to open up to his wife and children. Like Hank, we may have experienced difficulties in youth that obstruct our interactions with others as adults.

Jennifer suffered much physical and sexual abuse by family members. She developed an enormous capacity to detach from any sort of pain she might feel. "It was as if I left my body behind and numbed myself totally in order to not feel what was happening to me," she explained. "It was too much to bear. I didn't feel anything really. I'm not even sure I was there. I just somehow learned to check out. This is a wound that is hard to forget. I feel split into many pieces, and my healing will be a lifetime process."

With her ability to detach, she added the defense of intellectualizing. She can talk intelligently about anything, but she does not know how she personally feels about most subjects. For Jennifer, such behavior enabled her to survive childhood. However, now she has a difficult time moving beyond intellectualizing. This way of coping has left her lonely and friendless. She is often depressed without realizing why. Jennifer has found herself crying uncontrollably. She cannot grasp why life is so arduous; in fact, she does not want to continue living. The child within her will be silent no more. It is imperative that she begin to express the agony of the child within in order to be healed.

There is a part in many of us that cries for help, continues to experience great pain or longs for comfort. In our effort to lead a conventional life we do our best to deny ourselves access to that part. We banish that part in order to protect ourselves from the pain it contains.

The Manager Parts

As we determine to forget the negative experiences of youth, we develop another part whose job is to keep our exiles under control. The manager part presents our self to the world as though we were in complete control. We may have several manager sides that help us do what is needed to live as an adult. Our managers often come to our rescue through harsh and controlling efforts to keep us functioning and stabilized.

One client referred to her manager part as "Big Bertha" because she loomed so large in her life. Jenna's workmates and family saw her as competent in her external world, but in therapy she talked about her little girls who wanted to stay home, pull down the shades and rock all day in a rocking chair. We came to define these three little girls as the sad one, the angry one and the hurting one.

In therapy we paid attention to what these repressed voices

needed to say. The therapy office is a safe place to express the pain, anger and hurt of the past. Big Bertha was very critical of her little girls at first, trying to keep them from expressing their true feelings. But by and by she became more compassionate and understanding. Jenna availed herself of Big Bertha at the end of each session for strength to make it through another week without being overwhelmed by her exiled voices. Slowly, as we paid more attention to the little girl concerns, Big Bertha relinquished some of her control and Jenna could live at peace with herself.

The Firefighter Parts

Most of us have parts that act as firefighters. These pieces attempt to deal with the trauma and pain of our exiled parts through *acting out* or *acting in* behaviors. The firefighters rush in to extinguish the pain through distractions. While firefighters might numb the pain of the exiled parts momentarily, they cannot quench it. Compulsive-obsessive behaviors, substance abuse, religious fanaticism, overspending and undereating are some examples of firefighter activities.

When these extreme behaviors are working, the manager parts counter with similar extremes of overcontrol. They pronounce us guilty and shame us into "respectable" behaviors such as overwork, perfectionism and super-control of addictive appetites. Managers battle the destructive firefighter behaviors but fail to realize that control and cover-up tactics subvert the truth as well. The hidden pain continues to churn away inside. It becomes an unending, cyclical inner battle.

Since high school, Tim had been incapable of keeping a job for more than a year or two. The resulting shame led to excessive drinking. The drinking actually became the main reason he was fired again and again. Though he escaped through booze, in his sober moments his critical manager parts scolded him for being such a bad person. The self-defeating cycle worsened when he tried to commit suicide. Fortunately for Tim, he made a crucial U-turn at this point of no return. He joined a recovery program and faced his self-defeating exiled parts through honest exploration, challenged his manager parts in their unsuccessful efforts to control his behavior, and dealt directly with his firefighter escape tactics. After he started taking responsibility for himself and his actions with the support of Alcoholics Anonymous, he eventually developed a self he could respect again.

The Great Cover-Up
If you never learned how to feel, how to talk or how to trust, you are part of a great cover-up that inhibits intimacy. This is a huge barrier to knowing yourself, because the real person inside is blocked from expression. You become a physical frame living under the illusion that to be real is to be what *others* want from you. When you bring this false self forth, you only exhibit a partial self.

To complete your self you must integrate the pieces into a whole. Your exiled parts must be heard. Lost feelings must be found. Trust must be developed. The process is demanding, but achievable. You can feel again. Trust and nurture can be a part of your life. What is going on inside will begin to match what you show on the outside. Congruence can become a way of life.

How does a person organize complex parts into a whole? A starting point is to listen to your feelings rather than try to hide them. If a situation triggers sadness, acknowledge that the sadness is there for a good reason. In the beginning it may be only a vague awareness of a physical sensation that alerts you to feelings. But if you pay attention, this signal can put you in touch with the deeper meaning behind the sensation.

Have you ever noticed how some people allow a movie or a novel to touch their emotions, while others keep their emotions stifled or removed? Feelings that rise up during viewing or reading can indicate that one of your exiled parts identifies with a certain scene. If you suppress these feelings you will never understand what this part is trying to tell you. Listening gives you an opportunity to uncover the source of your exiled parts.

Acknowledging and embracing your feelings without panic will give you a chance of being congruent. Feelings are honorable because they let you recognize your true self and help others see more of you. That leads to healing and intimacy. Listening to various voices within helps you sort out the conflicts in the thinking and perspective of the parts. Knowing your internal parts as they make up your whole person empowers you to take responsible leadership.

Where Will This Lead?

You may wonder if it is essential to find the parts within or how much you need to delve into the past to know yourself. We believe it is an important way to discover and know yourself, if you are willing. We suggest you take time to reflect on your parts and listen to your story so you can uncover the pain and the control in order to determine what can be done.

What are the messages in your head about you? Do they limit your options in life? Can you live with the limitation? Are you comfortable with yourself? If you want to learn more about yourself, facing your inner parts should help. Self-awareness in such an intimate way is therapeutic.

Roger was highly cognitive, a go-getter and extremely successful in the business world. He intimidated many people because of his perfectionism. He dressed impeccably and never had a mussed hair on his head. But underneath that controlled person lurked a little boy deathly afraid of heights. Only his wife knew how absolutely panicked he felt about elevators and the elaborate plans he made to avoid high places.

One evening he met friends while at a convention in an unfamiliar city. They decided to have dinner, but Roger did not realize the restaurant was on the twentieth floor of the hotel. A glass elevator provided the only access. He opted to try hiding his phobia because he did not want anyone else to know he could not handle the situation. But once inside the elevator the little boy took control. He grabbed his wife and faced the elevator door, quivering, in her arms. At the top he grabbed onto the walls and became panic-stricken about how he would get back down.

Roger's friends were shocked to see this overly controlling man fall apart. After returning to the first floor, they spent the rest of the evening discussing the episode. Although flustered and embarrassed, Roger was relieved when his friends compassionately listened as he talked about his problem.

Later, in group therapy, Roger got in touch with his fearful child who was never able to satisfy the perfectionism demanded by his rigid parents. His fear had become a symptom of childhood inadequacies. His ability to handle his fear improved, and he became a more balanced person through the discovery of a full self.

The apostle Paul reminds us in Romans 7:15 that we neglect what we want to do, while we end up doing what we want to avoid. We are familiar with the parts of us that struggle with right and wrong. When our parts are polarized, they take on extreme behaviors. When our childhood has been harmful, the more damaged parts take longer to heal. Jesus, the One wounded for our transgressions, knows all about the hurts and pains of our exiled parts. He pays attention and urges us to come to him for healing. Jesus grieves when we use defenses to cover our pain. When we direct our inner voices to Jesus, he hears our cry and heals our wounds.

Old patterns of behavior can change. An expanded view of the self can lead to healing. If your exiled parts have been seriously wounded or you have a history of physical and sexual abuse, we recommend that you seek professional help. In a later chapter we will discuss how therapy can aid in knowing your inner self.

Knowing Your Unique Gifts

Some people have trouble identifying their healthy parts. If you struggle with self-esteem, the messages others heaped on you in earlier days may have become engrained in your mindset. Often these messages are severe: *You can't do anything right! What is wrong with you? Watch him, he'll break it!* When these thoughts have been internalized, they have the capacity to paralyze. The consequence can be an inability to function, even when you are actually capable.

We end up with a false feeling (shame) that comes from a false sense of self *(I'm stupid)*. We believe we deserve the shame we sense. We adapt the messages dictated to us by others and allow them to define us. We feel as though we do not measure up, are not good enough and will never be worthy. The frequent outcome is that we are stuck in a self-perception that is inaccurate.

I (Boni) remember growing up thinking I had no artistic talent. I now look at my high-school artwork and realize I had a false impression. However, the message became a self-fulfilling prophecy leaving its negative mark on my image. I allowed the perception to have a powerful grip into my adult years when I shied away from anything appearing to need an artistic hand, including decorating a cake, arranging a room or laying out a flowerbed. I may attempt such activities, but I assume I am not good at them. So I seek much advice, try to figure out what everyone else thinks is right and become nervous in the process. If someone questions my ideas, my stomach churns, and the *you're-not-good-enough* tape begins to roll. I have permitted the thoughts of others to rule. In the end, any gifts I may have in this area go unused.

Trustworthy friends may help us to overcome self-doubt and

realize our full potential. Often others see in us an ability we do not recognize in ourselves (my close friends tell me my artistic talent is above average). When a gift is encouraged, we may respond to the challenge and give it a whirl.

Marsha, a brilliant woman, had taught numerous adult Bible classes with great success. Watching her interact with her own children one morning, the Sunday-school superintendent asked if she would teach the class for preschoolers. Marsha appeared shocked. She could not imagine anything so far beyond her comfort zone. But she decided to pray honestly about the request. The next quarter she taught the tykes. They responded enthusiastically to her tender care and helpful teaching style. By the end of the following quarter parents complimented her on being one of best preschool teachers in the history of the church. For the next several years, Marsha gave her preschool class the benefits of all her wisdom, and they thrived. What a loss it would have been if she had never heeded the call to use her gift.

Our talents are all so different, yet 1 Corinthians 12 reminds us how necessary each individual is to the entire church body. When Ken joined his church, the scriptural knowledge of most of the members intimidated him. He confided his sense of inadequacy to the pastor, explaining that he felt out of place among so many knowledgeable people. Ken believed he could not be a leader or teacher. Unexpectedly, the pastor responded enthusiastically. "What we really need around here is someone who is willing to do the many tasks that never get done," the pastor said. "You are just who we need!" Ken's eyes lit up when he realized the pastor valued him and important assignments awaited him. Now Ken is always available if work is to be done. If meals need to be prepared, walls painted, gardens weeded or buildings repaired, Ken is the first to donate his time and talents. Other church members wonder how they survived without his help. Praise God for the person who discovers his gifts and is not afraid to use them.

Recently Ken expanded his gifts by starting to teach junior-high boys who respond to his relational style. He plays sports with the group and takes one boy out each week for a hamburger and soda. He is appreciated more than he ever could have imagined.

To know yourself you must answer those tough "who am I?" questions. The most difficult part may be taking the first step. Begin by making a list of all your known characteristics, describing yourself as best you can. Then make another list of all your likes and dislikes, including what you do well. Make the list positive, listing your skills no matter how small.

Honoring God

Knowing yourself is crucial to being intimate with yourself, and being intimate with yourself is necessary for healing. You cannot heal what you do not know. But how self-focused do we need to be in order to be healed? Where do we cross the line into self-centeredness?

Motive plays a large role in determining the answer. When we want to be all that God meant for us in our search for self-knowledge, God is pleased, blessed and honored. When our intention is self-glorification, we dishonor God and our preoccupation is an offense. God approves when we desire to know ourselves as we are truly known by the One who created us. On the other hand, if we continue in self-deception, negative talk and pseudohumility, we will never be the person God intended. Actually, a person is self-centered when he or she holds on to a concocted self-image instead of searching for the real self intended by God.

In this chapter we have suggested several methods of meeting yourself on a deeper level. You are God's cherished creation! Your most significant intimacy will be found in a personal knowledge of Jesus Christ. "The fear of the LORD is the beginning of wisdom, and the knowledge of the Holy One is insight" (Proverbs 9:10). Understanding God's creative power and our relationship to him is the beginning of self-knowledge for each one of us.

We also can learn much about ourselves through others. God did not intend for us to live in isolation, cut off from the rest of humanity. Our relationships will teach us much about ourselves if we let them. Others view us in ways we do not see ourselves. We receive direction and assistance in self-knowledge when we reveal ourselves to others. Knowing who you are in relationship to the significant people in your life expands your possibilities and is one of the most important ways to make needed changes. We will discuss this concept more fully in later chapters dealing with relationships.

We gain additional awareness of self when we examine our inner thoughts, feelings and memories. We can learn much by contemplating earlier experiences. If you are willing to spend time and energy to know the many parts that compose your past, you can work through barriers they have erected in your life. This is time-consuming. Unearthing the past can be painful and frightening, because sometimes you uncover horrible secrets. For many people the safest way to gain this kind of intimacy is with the help of a therapist, a committed friend, a small caring group or a spiritual director.

If you decide to know yourself at this deepest level, you will not be disappointed. We cannot gain true intimacy with self by keeping to ourselves in the here and now. Real healing occurs when we dare to look into the past in order to face the future with hope.

Giftedness is another important door to self-knowledge. Discovering the gifts God has given and venturing to develop them brings us to our full potential as God's chosen ones. No one feels complete, worthwhile and meaningful when not giving to others. That is why using your gifts to assist others is a part of your healing journey.

You are the one who needs to walk into the path of intimacy with yourself. Sometimes you will not enjoy what you find, but grace makes self-knowledge bearable. Only you can take the risk. Thank God you do not have to go alone. God has given us his Holy Spirit to be the presence of Christ in our healing process. This Spirit gives us the ability to look, to understand and to change. Do not ignore this third Person of the Godhead.

Questions for Thought

1. How does it feel to be known by God?

2. What parts of yourself do you attempt to keep from God?

3. What roles do you play in your relationships? Is this what you want?

4. What messages do you remember from childhood? Do you still believe them? Are they true?

5. Which of your gifts have you acknowledged and made available to others? Which are you afraid to acknowledge? Do you know why?

For Your Growth

Discover the various parts of your personality. Take the time to write a description of each. Draw a picture of each part, or find magazine pictures that depict your various sides. How is each helpful to you as a whole? How do they interact?

Describe your gifted self in as much detail as possible. List the areas where you excel.

4

HEALING
THROUGH MARRIAGE

After *many years of personal struggle, Carol finally broke* down and told her husband about the abuse she had suffered as a child. Would he think less of her? Would he blame her for her uncle's action? Would he think of her as dirty or undesirable now? Carol overcame her fears because she could no longer carry the burden alone. Through heavy tears, she divulged her secret past. She talked about the vacation that became a never-ending nightmare. She remembered being afraid to confide in anyone for fear that her uncle would carry out his threats.

As she talked, Frank began to boil. How could this have happened to Carol? And yet this explained so much of her behavior. What could he do now to help heal this wound? What would this mean for their marriage and their future? He felt shattered listening to the story.

But he never loved her more than at this moment.

That day Carol and Frank began a journey that proved difficult but indispensable as they reflected on their marriage vows of years earlier. They wanted healing for Carol and growth in their relationship. As Frank listened again and again to Carol's pain in the next months, he learned to know her in many new ways. He nurtured her in a manner that brought healing. She continued to disclose a hidden side that enhanced their relationship. Carol's lover and mate helped her heal.

Our marriages have the wonderful potential for being a healing force in our lives. That healing may come to partners individually or to the marital relationship itself. No earthly relationship has more possibility for intimacy than marriage. If we have a sturdy partnership and can risk being known by our spouse, opportunities for improved health abound.

Love at First Sight

Have you ever thought about when Adam and Eve met? What an intriguing, mysterious and exciting time it must have been as they first saw each other. "This at last is bone of my bones, and flesh of my flesh," Adam declared in Genesis 2:23.

Indeed, they were made for each other. Because Eve thought and felt as Adam did, they could connect at an intimate level. They had the capacity to understand, explore and discover each other. Their bodies had similarities, yet differences. Understanding her deepened his ability to know himself. Discovering Adam's identity gave Eve a fuller grasp of her individuality.

God appreciated Adam's requirement for a partner, an equal creature. Eve became the perfect companion. She, likewise, desired communion with one who was like her, made in God's image. Their linking involved a meeting of two minds, souls, bodies and emotions. And they became one flesh, naked and unashamed. This is intimacy in the purest form as God intended.

Some of us have experienced love at first sight with our spouses. For others, the love grew gradually into a rich and fulfilling relationship. Whichever path, intimacy did not happen naturally. Relationships should not be taken for granted. Marriages are not automatic healing environments. But if we are dedicated to that goal our association will be a powerful force for growth as individuals and as couples.

The Covenant Example

Marriage has the capacity to mirror the relationship we have with God. The potential for unconditional love, unmatched intimacy, unprecedented sharing, total commitment and steadfast faithfulness are clear parallels to our relationship with God.

This image is evident in Hosea. Yahweh persisted in calling the nation of Israel into intimacy and obedience, despite the infidelity of its inhabitants. Hosea showed how God presented himself as the faithful husband to the unfaithful wife in a resolute pleading. By wandering, she missed the blessing of an intimate relationship with her husband. As the people of Israel departed from God, they lost the source that sustained them. Yet God did not quit.

"In that day," declares the LORD,

"you will call me 'my husband' . . .

so that all may lie down in safety.

I will betroth you to me forever;

I will betroth you in righteousness and justice,

in love and compassion.

I will betroth you in faithfulness,

and you will acknowledge the LORD." (Hosea 2:16, 18-20 NIV)

Hosea's wife, Gomer, remains in an adulterous affair, yet he is ordered to pursue her. He is told to woo her and bring her to faithfulness so God can heal and bless her.

I will heal their disloyalty;
  I will love them freely . . .
They shall again live beneath my shadow,
  they shall flourish as a garden. (Hosea 14:4, 7)

The marriage relationship can demonstrate that same kind of persistence and unconditional love that God portrayed for us in Hosea. Linette and Todd are an example.

Linette grew up in a poverty-stricken family. As an adult she made financial security a priority. Todd wanted to provide the abundance that his wife seemed to crave. He tried to achieve wealth through a variety of get-rich-quick schemes, all of which ended in financial disaster. After Todd's investment opportunities had fizzled and Linette's security was shaken, they decided Linette should create a nest egg from her own funds. So part of the money she earned each month went into a savings account to be used only in emergencies. Then Todd stumbled upon what he viewed as a deal to beat all deals and needed some cash in a hurry. Secretly he withdrew Linette's savings, invested the money and hoped for the best. Unfortunately, the worst happened instead. All the money went down the tubes, devastating Linette. Her security disappeared, her trust in Todd had been shaken, and her love for him wavered.

The blessing came in their subsequent actions. Based on the covenant they had made at their wedding, Todd and Linette remained faithful to each other and used the crisis as a window of opportunity for restoration. Linette faced her fears of poverty and recognized the pressure her anxiety had placed on Todd. He, in turn, revealed his insecurity in the relationship and the resulting deceptive behavior. While many couples might have blamed each other and used the catastrophe as a perfect excuse to divorce, Linette and Todd renewed their commitment to love each other unconditionally. Both had been faithless in a way. Each needed healing. They grew in their commitment to each other and to God.

Extending Mercy

Someone once said, "Till death do us part should not be a life sentence." Indeed, some marriages seem to be nothing but hard work, painful disappointments and distressful interactions. In truth, everyone who is married inevitably fails at some point. We have clashes, we become disappointed, we offend, we violate trust, we blow it. We need grace!

When God looked at faithless Israel, he saw beyond their disobedience and focused on his love and commitment for them. God welcomes us back again and again in spite of our defiance. He accepts us because we belong to him. Forgiveness is part of God's character.

Similarly, when a husband and wife are connected by God to each other, forgiveness becomes integral to their relationship. God has every right to reject us in our sin and declare "Enough! I can take no more of your wayward behavior." Likewise, a spouse has the authority to divorce the mate caught in adultery. But those who have experienced the mercy of Christ also have the capacity to show mercy in human relationships. Because of the forgiveness shown to us, we can forgive. In Christ we have the ability to help heal others.

Safety First

While intimacy should be a mark of marriage, some relationships unfortunately are not safe enough for such sharing. To disclose part of yourself to another requires a certain amount of guardedness that does not necessarily become automatic with the marriage vows. Often I have heard fear expressed between partners when I ask them to share part of themselves with each other. "How do I know she won't use it against me later?" a husband asks. "If I tell him how I feel about this, he'll know how to hurt me," a wife responds. At this point, the union with so much potential for healing has become a standoff or battleground of unfair competition and fighting. Spouses sometimes have an intense fear of intimate loving because the capacity to harm each other is so great.

Safety begins with an unconditional love covenant, as we saw in the example of Hosea toward Gomer, as well as God toward humanity. If both partners are not committed to making the marriage work, however, they will hesitate to fully reveal their inner feelings. If I must wonder whether my mate will leave when I show the real me, I will take the safer route: hiding the parts that might be objectionable. A commitment to stay for better or worse is the sure foundation that allows for intimacy in marriage.

Respect and trust are crucial ingredients of unconditional love. No one is comfortable sharing with someone who ridicules or minimizes. A secure environment for self-disclosure is where feelings, ideas and thoughts are respected—and differences are permitted.

A safe relationship allows spouses to express themselves honestly. You will not hold back when you believe your partner has your best interests in mind and wants to know all about your identity. You will be excited to share your dreams with a spouse who enthusiastically supports your efforts to achieve these goals. You will feel safe when you do not need to worry about a jealous, withholding or competitive partner restricting your achievements. In fact, competition is unthinkable in a mutually empowering marriage because reaching personal goals is celebrated by both spouses. You will disclose your vulnerable places of doubts, fears and shame when you know your partner shows understanding rather than condemnation.

How is safety created in a marriage? First, safety needs to be pursued. You start with the fertile soil of unconditional love and acceptance. Next you add caring and encouraging nutrients. Then you wait. Realize that intimacy does not develop quickly. Give the space and time needed for mutual trust to develop. This can never be rushed. Each spouse must test the waters of safety. And, little by little, the marriage proves to be a protected place for deep sharing. The relationship becomes a haven of rest in a harried world; the marital bond becomes a shelter from the storms of life; spousal intimacy evolves into a healing force. The benefits reaped from being in a safe marital environment are the fruits of wisdom and wholeness. Put safety first and guard it with your life. Safety is the most precious gift to your marriage.

Naked and Unashamed

Lots of energy can be expended by a husband and a wife trying to hide from each other emotionally. Yet many couples choose to camouflage their feelings instead of being open and honest.

One reason for hiding is habit. In the outside world we all become proficient at wearing masks and concealing our real feelings and thoughts. We also may try to fool our spouses. Reaching the point of emotional nakedness with another is risky. To be so open means sharing our innermost being, fears, delights, concerns, doubts, opinions and ideas with our partner. Being known can elicit tremendous fear. We fear being judged, losing love or being rejected. So instead of intimate interaction being exhilarating and comforting, it is a time of excruciating insecurity.

If judgment or rejection is the consequence of sharing yourself openly, you will pull back to protect yourself. If overwhelming expectations or blame is the result, you will stop risking further exposure. Under these circumstances, intimacy is personal suicide.

If reactions such as these have shattered your relationship, the first corrective step should be to acknowledge and deal with the distrust that has occurred. Mending is possible only when spouses can establish enough trust to invest themselves again. The pattern of covering up rather than opening up is common in marriages. Unless the problem is admitted, distancing maneuvers will continue to destroy intimacy.

Behind the Mask

One of the frightening aspects of showing our true identity is that our spouse might not like what is seen or heard. As with other relationships, we worry that we will not be acceptable without our mask. The possibility of rejection is too difficult to bear. Only when we are confident that we will be accepted regardless of our thoughts and feelings will we risk self-disclosure. This does not mean we are proud of what lies hidden under that mask. But we desperately need our spouse to say, "I see who you are and I accept the ugly parts as well as the lovely parts."

John had never realized that his wife, Vickie, suffered panic attacks regularly. He perceived her behavior as moodiness, but he did not know how to respond. When panic struck, Vickie confused the real problem by being irritable or isolating herself. She considered the façade preferable to letting John think anything was *really* wrong with her. She knew John disapproved of weak women. Her overriding fear was that John would discover her weakness and eventually leave her.

Vickie ultimately sought therapy and invited John to a session to disclose her panic attacks. John greeted the truth with relief. As her irritability had increased, he had imagined a much worse problem. As she shared, their relationship matured. Together they worked on an approach to overcoming fear that helped Vickie tremendously. John grew too as he figured out that his expectations for Vickie originated from his own fears and inadequacies. He accepted Vickie for who she was, rather than trying to mold her into what he wanted her to be.

Acceptance is amazing. We may fear that our spouse will not accept us when we age or if we become debilitated with physical or emotional illness. If that is the case, early in marriage we may keep our distance in order to protect ourselves from the pain of that fearful day. Such conduct means we miss the intimacy that turns into deep love.

The following exchange is from an essay by Richard Selzer called "Lessons from the Art of Surgery." The physician describes a consultation with a patient and her boyfriend after the patient had undergone surgery that left her mouth deformed. It beautifully portrays the quality of unconditional love and acceptance that can develop in marriage.

The young woman speaks. "Will my mouth always be like this?" she asks. "Yes," I say, "it will. It is because the nerve was cut."

She nods, and is silent. But the young man smiles.

"I like it," he says. "It is kind of cute."

All at once I know who he is. I understand, and I lower my gaze. One is not bold in an encounter with a god.

Unmindful, he bends to kiss her crooked mouth, and I am so close I can see how he twists his own lips to accommodate to hers, to show her that their kiss still works. (Quoted in Bernie S. Siegel, *Love, Medicine and Miracles* [New York: Harper & Row, 1986], p. 190)

Sexual Closeness

Many people immediately think of sex when they hear the word *intimacy*. More people are afraid of emotional intimacy than sexual intimacy. Impersonal sex is less threatening than intimate intercourse or creating an ongoing emotional love connection with your spouse. There is much more to intimacy than being sexual.

Males traditionally have been accused of equating sexual intercourse with marital intimacy. Females, on the other hand, are stereotyped as equating emotional closeness with intimacy. For the married couple, both are important. The physical act of intercourse is the byproduct of the love expressed between two people who know and love each other. Psychological knowing and tenderness engenders physical knowing and tenderness. It allows spouses to present themselves in mutual abandonment. Expressing the sexual self without shame or hesitation is an important form of self-disclosure.

Many of us have grown up with a negative sexual view of ourselves. Men often are overwhelmed by the expectations put on them to be strong and in control emotionally. Women often carry around messages about being too emotional or irrational. Both genders can enter marriage with secret doubts about their sexuality or their attractiveness to the opposite sex.

These situations present real opportunities for healing within the sexual relationship. New possibilities emerge as couples share fears with each other. For example, affirming the tender side of your husband or encouraging your wife to take the sexual initiative is healthy in expanding concepts of masculinity and femininity.

Carolyn never had looked at herself naked. She could not even tolerate the thought. Checking out some illustrations in an anatomy book was the limit for her. Even though she was physically attractive, Carolyn was ashamed of her body.

Vinny came from a strong Italian family where men traditionally expressed macho sexual desires. The affection he actually felt for his wife embarrassed him. He loved being sexual with her, but he also found great pleasure in being tender without sex. He believed real men should not act this way, so he hid his feelings.

Nancy wondered how being a Christian and being sexual could be compatible. She thought of sex as dirty: Christian wives have to engage in intercourse, but they are not expected to *enjoy* it. Yet when her husband, Michael, tenderly touched her, she admitted she liked it. Were those passions wrong? What would Michael think if he knew she enjoyed the erotic part of marriage?

In each of these cases, so much could be gained if the couples would begin to share their feelings willingly. They could begin to relate to each other in ways that acknowledge all parts of each person. They would begin by listening empathically and actively. They would allow opportunity for each to explore their thoughts and feelings regarding sexual concerns. They would state their acceptance of their partner, in spite of hangups. They might look for active ways of enhancing their sexual relationship to counter dysfunctional thoughts and behaviors. They would find ways of noticing the sexuality in each other and celebrating it as God's good gift. These actions would bring out greater intimacy between them.

Sexual intimacy is an opportunity for spirit, mind, emotions and body to work together to further the health of each partner. It cannot happen without a safe emotional connection already in place. But if that part of our relationship is intact, physical openness follows.

The Value of Marriage

Have you ever considered your marriage an investment? If it is true, why don't the intensity and intentionality of our courting days continue? At a weekly breakfast meeting of six men shortly after Valentine's Day, two confessed that their wives had been bothered when they did not receive a card or gift. All six of the men had struggled in one way or another with expectations and pressures surrounding Valentine's Day.

After some initial joking about media hype and agitated wives, the discussion took a more serious tone. Why was expressing appreciation on this particular day so difficult? What did their discomfort and insecurity indicate on a deeper level? Why were their wives so hurt by their failure to commemorate romance and intimacy? One of the younger men asked a simple question that spurred them all to consider the level of intimacy in their marriages: "Why don't we invest in our marriage relationship the way we invest in other things that matter to us, like our work or our car?" That is a sobering question for husbands and wives alike. Each man affirmed that he wanted to feel valued and appreciated by his wife.

Where we invest ourselves is where our commitment lies. We put time and effort into what is important to us, and we take a great deal of satisfaction in expending energy on what we consider worthwhile.

The eventual return on our investments is what makes them increasingly valuable.

One reward of devoting time and effort in our marriage is the level of intimacy we can develop in the emotional, intellectual, sexual, aesthetic, creative, recreational and spiritual aspects of the relationship. Shared experience and expression in each of these areas strengthen our marriage bond.

Speaking at a young couples' Sunday-school class, Dean and Doreen Smiley told how mutual caring brought vitality to their marriage. "We've experienced marital intimacy by (1) finding creative solutions to problems that are unique to us, (2) expanding our thinking after expressing different points of view, (3) enjoying God's great creation through a walk on the beach or a view from a mountaintop, (4) praying through a painful crisis in our family, (5) forgiving each other after a communication breakdown, (6) working together on raising our family and completing projects on our home, (7) feeling emotionally connected after a vulnerable time of sharing, (8) soaking in the ecstasy of our sexual oneness, (9) experiencing a moving spiritual moment together and (10) recommiting ourselves to each other on our twenty-fifth wedding anniversary." Indeed, they are reaping rewards of intentional marriage investment. Their commitment has been a storehouse of plenty helping them through the dry spells and crises.

Life's Distractions
Numerous distractions make investment in marriage a major challenge. We all know men and women struggling with the demands of climbing the corporate ladder. The sacrifices they make during the climb are huge. Some devote an equal amount of time to the care of children; others take on one task after another. Some even use kingdom work to prevent them from marital intimacy. In all these cases, investment in marriage becomes minimal because everything

else takes higher priority. Spouses chug along like two trains running on parallel tracks. They never connect until disaster strikes—and then it may be too late.

We must find a way to live in tandem, to bring and to keep our lives together in vital connection. Unity develops as each partner devotes energy to the partnership, increasing the mate's growth through a dynamic interchange of giving and receiving.

The Balswicks' marriage became a crucible of sorts with the diagnosis of our son Jeff's bone cancer. Such stress brings out the worst and the best in people, and we were no exception. We experienced an unbelievable shakeup in our lives. Yet our marriage had been solidly built during the previous fifteen years, and the intimacy established in many areas provided a strength that allowed us to stand together.

We had no secrets to hide. My husband, Jack, sat in the car that day as I screamed "why?" questions to God. Jack knew my pain at its deepest level, for he loved Jeff as intensely as I did. I agonized with the helplessness Jack felt after his last camping trip with Jeff. We expressed our pain, hurt and anger differently, and this was OK because we had learned to view our differences as resources rather than liabilities. United in our individual strengths, we walked through each stage of the illness as honestly as we knew how. Sometimes we struck out at each other, because a life-threatening illness demands difficult decisions. But grace and forgiveness saw us through the grueling five months.

We lovingly cared for Jeff in the privacy of our home during the last month of his life. We spoke openly with him about his impending death and God's promises of everlasting life. We experienced spiritual comfort when Jeff told us about an angelic visit the night before he died. Jack sat beside Jeff as he died in his sleep.

During those trying months we drew closer to each other as a couple. We experienced God's peace in our love. We knew what it was to love our son intimately and also to lose one we loved so dearly. But how much more would the loss have been had we not risked loving him while we had the chance? Fortunately we had built our marriage to a level of trust and intimacy that could sustain the crisis. This could not have been done in the midst of the dilemma.

Intimacy Lost

Some relationships have suffered so much hurt or neglect that the desire for intimacy and healing is gone. Facing that degree of distance is painful. You may even dread looking at your spouse. Sentiments of love have been overtaken by feelings of hurt. If this is the case, the risk of being intimate is frightening. Finding the courage to approach each other comes only from your desire to be obedient to Christ.

Reestablishing safety will require special diligence. The first step is to institute clear ground rules. In a relationship full of hurt and anger, sharing can easily escalate into a free-for-all, so professional help may be needed. A well-trained marital therapist can provide the safe environment that allows you to address issues in a healing manner.

Healing the hurt of broken trust is just the beginning. You will have to struggle with many personal questions. Did I distort the situation with misinformation? Did I keep secrets that destroyed intimacy? Did I break vows? Did I keep the relationship as my first priority? Did I take the interests and needs of my spouse seriously? Did I meet my obligations? What did I do to produce happiness and intimacy between us? Do I disassociate sex from emotions? Did I seek my spouse's well-being? Did I encourage my mate's growth and fulfillment? Did I have the capacity for feeling and understanding? Did I share and keep my promises? Did I minimize or demean my spouse? Did I listen, care, accept, invest and treat my spouse as my equal?

These are tough questions to ask when intimacy seems lost. Yet when addressed truthfully, these questions can be the beginning of healing in you and in your marriage. God will bless your efforts and renew your hope.

A Suitable Helper

Marriage can be one of the greatest resources for personal change. The goal is not to change our spouse into someone who will meet our own needs. That would be controlling, possessive and narcissistic. Rather, in the process of being known we are opened, exposed and seen by our spouse. When we become vulnerable to each other, we have a tremendous capacity either to hurt or to heal. No wonder giving of ourselves in this way takes such grace and trust.

In the intimacy of this relationship we see ourselves as we really are: betraying trust, lacking faith, acting dishonorably, wanting our own way or tending to be cruel, indifferent, thoughtless or jealous. Indeed, we take a great risk when we show our true colors to our spouse.

But healing comes for partners who establish a covenant of trust. When spouses are committed to each other for better or worse, when they cherish their differentness and uniqueness, when they empower one another, when they confront as well as listen to each other, when grace is the basis for forgiving, they can be healed.

Intimacy between partners brings repair of the soul. Here my most loving partner not only allows me to be myself but persists in asking questions that reveal even more of my identity. In the intimacy of marriage, I can dare to face myself. And with the love and commitment of my spouse behind me I find the courage to change. How wise our Lord is to draw two together, to make them helpers suitable for each other.

Questions for Thought

1. What is meant by a safe relationship for a husband and wife? How do you provide a secure environment for your spouse?

2. Are there areas in your marriage where you have extended or received mercy? What was that like?

3. Describe the investment you have made in your marriage. What have been the gains or losses of that investment?

4. What were some qualities mentioned in this chapter that have kept you from intimacy as a couple? Are you aware of others?

5. Together, answer the questions in the "Intimacy Lost" section of this chapter. Share your answers in the safety of a therapist's office or with another trusted couple.

For Your Growth
How has your sexual relationship been a healing force? Think of specific ways to encourage the emotional and spiritual aspects of your sexual intimacy. Write these ideas down, and promise to do one each week to enhance your emotional and spiritual life as a couple.

5

HEALING &
FAMILY LIFE

I *(Boni) remember an evening a few years ago when my daughter* Karlie came to me in tears because of a dreadful incident at school—a conflict with a close friend. She needed to talk about what had happened, so I used my best listening skills. The conversation, I thought, went quite well. After about forty-five minutes I felt pleased about being such a good mom. But as she got up to leave, Karlie said, "Thanks for listening, Mom, but I sure wish you would give me some advice. Do you really get paid for that?"

A fourteen-year-old girl who prepared to leave my office also had misgivings about her mother. "It's off to 'quality time' with my mom," she said somewhat disgustedly. "I wish she would give this up. We'll probably decorate cookies or something."

As much as we try, intimacy does not always work as well as we expect. Helpful advice for adults is not always appropriate for children. A wonderful experience for young children may be a real bore to teenagers. Intimacy does not always fall into place naturally, even for parents who long to develop close, healthy family relationships.

So What's New?

"Hi, Mom, I'm home!" is not so common a greeting anymore. "Is anybody home?" is far more common. Most kids come home from school to an empty house, grab a snack and plop down in front of an impersonal television set. We wonder where all the family togetherness has gone. During a typical day family members do not find time to talk, listen or share an important event in their lives. Closeness is rare in modern society.

Nostalgia teaches that families had more time with each other in the good ol' days. But families who happened to sit around the same dinner table did not necessarily share intimate details of their lives. Despite the cozy vision we have of the closely knit family of yesteryear, members who were physically near each other much of the time often could be emotionally detached.

One day when I rhapsodized about the ideal life of the farm family with a Midwestern friend, he retorted, "You got that all wrong! My father spent more time with the cows than he did with me. Just because we worked side by side doing farm work didn't mean we were an emotionally close family."

Closely Knit Families

Textbooks refer to an overdependency among family members as *enmeshment*. It is as though a brother does not know where his arm ends and his sister's arm begins. In enmeshed families, members must think alike, feel the same emotions and hold the same values. In my family, for instance, my daughter pointed out that through certain statements I sometimes tried to impose illogical decisions on the rest of the family. I would say such things as "It's cold. You better put on a sweater," or "I feel tired; we'd better go to bed." Was I speaking for me or for everybody? I assumed my thoughts or feelings should be what the rest of my family thought and felt too. Some may call that closeness; others may consider it strangulation. But nobody would define it as intimate connection.

Enmeshment and intimacy are actually poles apart. What may appear to an outsider as closely knit really may be quite suffocating to the insider. An enmeshed family demands conformity, stifling the uniqueness and creativity of individual members. For example, if someone expresses a difference of opinion, the rest of the family immediately questions that person's loyalty. Soon individual family members learn they must suppress true feelings and independent ideas in order to stay in the good graces of the family.

The enmeshed family lives under the false impression that intimacy cannot tolerate individuality or self-identification. In actuality the enmeshed family is extremely fragile, because no one is permitted to upset the delusion of unity. Belonging and loyalty are highly valued qualities in families of all cultures, but in an enmeshed system these dimensions take on a life of their own to control members in a negative way. Extreme dependency requires blind loyalty, while intimacy, on the other hand, requires honest expression. Differentiation means family members can freely express thoughts or feelings without being labeled disloyal. In fact, differentiated family members are loyal to their family out of choice rather than out of obligation or pressure.

A person does not have the capacity to separate without first belonging. Belonging and separation are two sides of the same coin. When enmeshment is viewed as the ideal, members are given the wrong impression of closeness. Eventually that impression makes it hard for them to know how to establish genuine closeness with others inside or outside the family.

The Best Solutions

In families that work well, the ideas of all are accepted as valid, and each person's feelings are recognized as important. Feelings and ideas are not repressed or denied for the sake of family loyalty, but are encouraged for clarity and understanding. A request for change is regarded as reasonable and will be considered in light of the best interests of all concerned.

Families that pay attention to the feelings, ideas and needs of each person show respect for differentiation. When a teenager says, "I'm sick of this. I want to drop out of school," parents are not trapped into taking the statement literally. There is no need to minimize the turmoil the child is experiencing by responding with "Drop out of school? You can't do that! What could you be thinking?" Instead parents look beyond the actual words and pay attention to the underlying problem: "You sound discouraged. What's going on at school that's upsetting you?" This leads to further understanding and expands the possibilities of solutions for the teenager.

When parents react negatively to emotions, their children will feel forced to keep their feelings in check. They soon learn it is easier to be dishonest about feelings and keep their thoughts to themselves. On the other hand, families that share their feelings with each other are learning how to be intimate. When emotions are handled with care, members sense it is safe to be honest. They will risk sharing fears, hopes, disappointments, dreams, frustrations and joys when they know they will be received and taken seriously. They learn that to be vulnerable is to be comfortable with intimacy.

How Things Change

Most families tend to be somewhat reluctant to change, but effective families will negotiate adjustments for the good of all concerned. Any individual suggestions about family change will be taken seriously, discussed and implemented when consensus is reached.

Sometimes change will mean compromise; other times a new and better way will be wholeheartedly embraced. In all cases, individuals are valued, no matter what age, and each has power to introduce suggestions. Final decisions are made by the entire family, but even if a proposal is not fully implemented, the ideas have been understood and members will have a new sensitivity to the issues that concern a particular member. In this way the family already has adjusted, because the dialogue itself has brought change.

Closeness grows when a family sets aside a regular time to be together. In a cordial and relaxed atmosphere, family members can make themselves vulnerable by expressing their points of view and listening to those of other members. Relating to each other without pretension promotes honesty and freedom to disclose at deeper levels. There is no need to monitor or restrain ideas out of fear about what others think, for family members will be in the habit of hearing each other out, no matter how crazy or ridiculous the ideas seem. Intimacy among family members allows each one to let the others know what is going on so they can respond with covenant love and grace.

A Circle of Love

Covenant love is a unilateral commitment that parents consciously make to their children. This commitment should become an ongoing way of life for everyone in the family. When parents bring children into their household, there is no way to anticipate what each unique child will bring or need. Unconditional love means that parents and even siblings promise to love the newest member even before he or she can love in return.

Both of our families had the privilege of adopting Korean children. Sarah arrived in the Piper family as a six-month-old baby, recognized by an enormous smile by day and a shrieking cry by night. The adjustments of a geographical move, plus unfamiliar faces and surroundings, caused anxiety. The whole family vowed to respond to Sarah's needs despite the ear-piercing screams. Her six-year-old brother, Aaron, crawled into her crib in the early morning hours to cuddle her. Her four-year-old sister, Karlie, also held her tenderly. They determined to do their part in the family commitment to love Sarah unconditionally. All worked together so Sarah could feel loved. Now a beautiful sixteen-year-old girl, Sarah is the one bringing warmth and comfort to family and friends.

Joel came into the Balswick home at age ten, unsure of this ready-made family. All of us had to adapt to his entry into our family. It was not love at first sight, because he initially resisted our attempts at physical affection, even though he seemed to want desperately to be held. We understood his fear of connecting: he had been abandoned and orphaned five years earlier. His natural inclination to aloofness broke my heart, because I wanted to bring him immediately into our intimate circle of family love. Still, we had reservations. Our family of three had experienced the loss of a son/brother, and we had fears and questions about letting this stranger into our circle.

Intimacy does not happen instantly or automatically. We had to discover ways to communicate our love through faithful acts of caring. We had to accept conditions that existed and hope that intimate connection would develop. Now when my twenty-six-year-old son walks through the door, puts his arm around me and says, "I love you, Mom," I am delighted we took the risk.

A Gift from God

How does a family accept a new member? Whether it is a colicky baby or one who rarely cries, a perfectly formed newborn or one with spina bifida, a biological or adopted infant, we receive a child as a gift. This little person is a precious child of God who has been entrusted to our care. An intimate family knows how to respond faithfully to the unique needs of a new baby. They know how to bond by giving themselves sacrificially to the newborn. This is the purest form of love between humans and comes closest to the unconditional love God offers us.

This year Judy's nephew Bret and his wife, Terry, gave birth to their third daughter, Corinne. After a speedy delivery, the medical staff conferred in low voices as they examined the baby. Bret saw his child and recognized the signs of Down syndrome. He immediately carried his little daughter to her mother without apprehension, because he knew Terry would love her regardless. The three of them embraced, bonded in a circle of love. Their profound faith served as a testimony to the doctors and nurses and has continued to give them courage through ongoing medical treatments. They believe with all their hearts that God is in control and will give them all they need to be loving parents to Corinne throughout her life. They know raising her will not always be easy, but with the support of family and friends they also are confident they will joyfully love her forever.

Conflict: Life's Fertilizer

Family conflict is inevitable. Even the most warm and loving households deal with disagreements because the personalities and perspectives of each family member are unique. Family therapist Carl Whitaker has said, "Conflict should rightly be considered the fertilizer of life. While not always fragrant, it's crucial for optimal growth" (Whitaker and Bumberry 1988:200). Family members actually drift apart when there is a lack of conflict, or apathy. If we do not care enough about each other to grapple with our differences, we are like a fallow field. In the dance of life we experience a recurring theme of coming together, moving in counterpoint and rejoining to keep in step with the music. The challenge is to learn how to dance without stepping on each other's toes.

We Fail Each Other

The family consists of unique individuals with different needs, gifts, desires and rates of personal and physical growth. Living together in unity is demanding. Members undoubtedly will face conflicts. Becoming involved in the lives of others means you are aware of both positive and negative traits.

Being human, we will fail, disappoint and hurt each other. We will need to forgive each other over and over. We will rub each other the wrong way; friction is a natural outcome of living in intimate relationships. Broken promises will remind us of the pain of breached trust. But only when our conflicts are brought into the open and dealt with will we be able to reclaim our intimate connection.

Intimacy does not mean there is absence of conflict—just the opposite. Those we love are the object of our strongest feelings, positive and negative. When we care about each other, conflicts bring us into passionate clashes that actually increase our intimate knowing. Most people mistakenly believe that conflict destroys love, but actually contention can increase intimacy. When we confront the reasons for our fighting and the rough places are made smoother, closeness follows.

How Families Can Empower Their Members

A healing family environment provides opportunities for each member to recognize individual gifts and to fulfill potential. An empowering family points each member toward maturity through responsible actions, rather than doing for them what they should do for themselves. We will be inspired to reach our greatest potential when we believe in the giftedness in each other. When we overfunction for someone who is underfunctioning, we imply, "You are incapable, let me do it for you. You can't succeed without me." The message the person needs to hear instead communicates our belief in individual ability. "Go ahead and try" and "I think you can do it" are attitudes that encourage people to reach higher.

Empowering is similar to discipling. If we want to empower people to perform a task, we should teach and equip them with skills. Judy remembers when Joel began to answer the phone in the Balswick house. He never seemed to interpret a message straight, and that irritated us. However, we eventually realized we never had given proper instructions for answering the phone. We assumed a ten-year-old would naturally know how, but Joel had never had practice. Besides, he had only started to learn English! We had hindered his empowerment. So we took time to teach him what to say and how to write down phone numbers. Then we rehearsed until he felt comfortable. From that day forward he felt in control whenever he took messages. He answered the phone with enthusiasm, his language skills improved, and he gained confidence in relating to other people. We appreciated his efforts, and everyone benefited.

Parents who empower know how to encourage, affirm, guide and keep correction to a minimum. They understand that children learn best from their mistakes if blunders are considered an opportunity for growth. The mother who wants her eight-year-old son to choose his own clothes for school in order to develop a sense of personal style and responsibility must be prepared to ignore bizarre combinations from time to time. Advice can be given about color schemes and styles, but if the child is to be empowered, Mom cannot continue to choose outfits each day. Peer feedback will soon help the child to learn what fads and color combinations to avoid.

Rules That Empower
Parents must provide clear guidelines and appropriate rules for family conduct. Rules work best when all members have input, rather than when parents merely establish and enforce the rules. Establishing rules together makes siblings accountable to each

other as well as to their parents. Rules must be perceived as being in the best interest of the family, not simply for the convenience of the parents. Keeping rules then means that the family is cooperating for the good of the whole. When each member can participate in chores and family decisions, everyone becomes an integral part of the family.

Coming together to decide family matters shows that everyone counts. Family members feel empowered when their opinions and ideas are seriously considered. The kids will keep parents accountable for decisions about family activities, such as vacations, holiday plans and weekly family nights. It is to the family's advantage if all members have a voice in decision-making and problem-solving.

When someone believes in you and comes beside to support and encourage, you respond with warm feelings. Think for a moment about a couple of people who empowered you as you grew up. What did they do to empower you? Take a moment to bask in the fond memories and say a prayer of thanks for those special people. Being empowered brings us healing, and empowering others brings them healing. Have you empowered anyone lately?

Families That Harm

Families have the capacity to destroy as well as heal. Childhood is our learning ground for intimacy. What happens or fails to happen in these early years has a great effect on our ability to trust others as we grow up. The barriers we erect as adults usually are the result of insufficient connection and bonding with our primary caretakers during childhood. Children who are loved, encouraged and nurtured grow into healthy adults. Youths who are neglected, oppressed and rejected turn out to be emotionally damaged adults.

Pat grew up in a negative atmosphere. As an adult, she uses her artistic talent to a small degree at church. Her mind is sharp, but she is reluctant to share an opinion in a group. The only place she is really comfortable is working with children, and then only if no adults are watching.

I (Boni) often wonder what this woman would be like if she were free of the negative voices from childhood: "What a stupid picture! What is that supposed to be?" "Your sister is the smart one. We just hope you make it through high school." These statements had long-lasting effects. The adage "Sticks and stones can break my bones, but words can never hurt me" is a lie. Unless we are released from damaging messages, we tend to fulfill them. We internalize the opinions of others, even if they are spoken in jest. If Pat brought up the subject today her parents would say, "Of course we liked your picture. No, we didn't mean that you were stupid." Unfortunately, children do not always ask. Instead they allow thoughtless words to leave a wrong impression in their minds.

Pat has been too frightened to use her gifts openly. With negative thoughts such as *My work is not good enough, I'm too dumb to express my opinion* and *Everyone would see I'm no good if I spoke or if they saw my work,* she leads a limited life. She has retained the fears and negative messages of childhood.

Broken Lives

Abusive family systems violate the body, heart and soul of children. Adults who were abused as children need to work out the pain of their destructive families. Safe relationships that encourage growth rather than those that keep them trapped in painful memories are needed if they are to flourish as adults.

Recently I talked with Dan. He was not sexually or physically abused while growing up, but he was neglected. He now experiences severe depression, low self-esteem and recurring suicidal thoughts. He sadly declared that he had no relationship with his mother. She was cold, never expressing love or affection. She never joked, played or even argued with her son. Dan grew up feeling as though he did not even exist. He emerged from this destructive family severely damaged.

Eventually, Dan married a woman much like his mother. She eagerly told him how to think, what to wear and how to organize his day. *What more could he want?* she thought. Several years into their marriage, she was shocked to find her husband on the brink of suicide. She had thought her take-charge influence would contribute happiness, but it had the reverse effect. Sometimes I call Dan "the invisible man," because no one notices him and he barely sees himself. His wife could give him everything but love, the gift he needed most.

It is not uncommon for people to marry a partner who represents the unhappy experience in their family of origin. Sadly, these marriages usually fail. Dan's wife tried to do the thinking and acting for him, but that only increased his feelings of worthlessness. One's spouse can never totally compensate for the deficits of one's childhood. Each person must find a way to recognize and overcome deficiencies in order to transcend them.

Betrayal

I also counseled Nathan, a man who had been physically abused severely by his parents and sexually abused by a friend of his father. His upbringing had not provided healing or nurturing. Unfortunately, neither did his marriage. After starting therapy he told his wife about the abuse he suffered as a child. She reacted with disgust and heaped insults upon him. She questioned his manhood and threatened to leave. Her inability to help delayed his healing tremendously. She could not tolerate his need for emotional intimacy and only added to his humiliation. He had no place of safety, nowhere to share his burden.

The family has enormous power to be emotionally destructive, both for adults and children. But if a family has developed real intimacy among members and can *contain* their pain, true healing is available for those in need. When we are a "container" for someone else's pain, we help them keep the effects of the pain limited. We help them stay focused on the root cause of the pain, rather than allowing it to run amok and contaminate all relationships. We accomplish this by validating their feelings, maintaining confidentiality and assuring them we want to help them share the pain in a safe environment.

Jaimie had been sexually abused as a child. Unlike Nathan in our former example, she found that telling her husband was helpful. Devon worked closely with her to rebuild her trust of men. He nurtured her in a gentle, nonsexual way to advance healing. He remained patient on those days when she could do nothing but cry. On other days he taught her to be playful. Devon took an active role in Jaimie's recovery, and eventually the blessing returned to him. As her deepest hurts healed, Jaimie could love her husband in a way she had been incapable of before.

Devon's unconditional love and ability to be intimate became evident. He bore his wife's pain and simultaneously empowered her in the healing process.

Sometimes a surrogate or extended family as well as a spouse and children can supply the right environment for healing oppressive images of the past. No system is more important or more basic to the healing of a human being—and none taken more for granted—than the family.

This works with children too. Several years ago I (Boni) treated a young boy, Kenny, who had been molested by a neighbor. His family already knew how to be intimate. Their closeness proved to be an incredible source of strength for him and his family. They candidly discussed the abuse in family sessions. They cried with their abused member on some days and acted as a source of strength on others. Kenny's brothers rebuilt his sense of self-worth and never stopped believing he could recover from the pain and humiliation.

His father talked openly about sexuality and listened to his son's doubts. The process lasted longer than anyone wanted and was grueling at times. But Kenny had a caring family not about to let him suffer on his own. Their ability to empathize helped him to overcome what could have been debilitating abuse.

Thankfully, this family had developed intimacy skills before the crisis. Love among the members enabled them to support each other significantly. When family members experience unconditional love, when faithful and proper bonding takes place, when trust has been built through caretaking, children are ready for the empowering process.

This process can start at a young age. When that solid foundation is in place, even preschoolers will risk doing things for themselves, stretching their limits of creativity and gaining self-confidence. Children who learn the fundamentals early often desire to be responsible and grow into maturity more quickly.

Parent God: Our Model

We bonded to God through Christ with a merciful love that continually draws us by grace. We believe we can depend on that covenant of love and know that God has our ultimate good in mind. Part of God's love is in establishing rules. We understand the law is for guidance, keeping us dependent on the power of the Holy Spirit for the ability to obey. When we fail, we are forgiven and restored, building further intimacy and love for God. What a perfect model for family life God provides!

The family that lives by law alone blocks intimacy between members. But grace in family life leads to intimacy. Even though we know we deserve punishment, we are treated with exceptional kindness instead. As a child friend said recently, "The thing I like most about my mom is she gives me breaks." Intimacy requires this attitude. Working alongside our children, giving warmth and attention, being alert to feelings, thoughts and spiritual needs, is possible because of the grace we have received in Christ Jesus.

Empowered children know who they are as God's children. They know they are made in the image of God. Their identity and confidence come from that knowledge. As they put their trust in God they know they are esteemed and cherished by God as a unique creation with a unique purpose and meaning.

Children who are loved, accepted, encouraged, heard and helped will have a capacity for intimacy. They will be responsible for themselves and learn how to meet their own needs. When parents interact with their children, respecting their views and needs, the household is marked by negotiability as well as accountability. Flexibility is a mark of any healthy family.

The family whose members know they are loved by God is the ideal setting to learn and practice self-disclosure and honest sharing. Family members need not be secretive. They can be unashamed. In an environment of loving, serving, forgiving and knowing each other, each member comes into healing.

Questions for Thought

1. What areas of your family life promote enmeshment? How can you encourage a healthy self-identification?

2. Which feelings are acceptable and which are unacceptable in your family? Is conflict a fertilizer that causes growth in your family? If not, what can you do about it?

3. How are new members received or released in your family? Consider birth, adoption, marriage, death.

4. What are some empowering behaviors that happen in your family?

For Your Growth

Hold a family meeting in which members take turns as leader. The leader makes certain everyone has an opportunity to air ideas and express feelings about any matter that arises. Attempt to negotiate rules and traditions as a family. Each member should state one aspect of family life he or she would like to change. Brainstorm ideas about how to make needed changes. Take sufficent time for positive interaction. For instance, ask each person to list three things about the family she or he enjoys. Finally, plan a fun time for the family each week. Everyone should have a part in deciding what to do. End the meeting with prayer for each other and the family as a whole.

6

HEALING IN FRIENDSHIP

As *a twelve-year-old, I was sitting on the porch glider one warm* Memorial Day evening when my mother came to the screen door and spoke words I had been dreading: "Boni, Arlene just died."

We had spent the day picnicking with friends. All day I had felt guilty about enjoying myself so much. With my best friend in all the world dying, it did not seem right. And now the phone call had come. The knot in my stomach grew tighter as I strained to listen. I had anticipated the arrival of the sad news, yet the pain gripped me. Even now, thirty-five years later, the knot comes, the tears well up behind my eyes, and I realize how much I miss my childhood friend.

Friendship is a wonderful gift, yet so often in our culture it goes unappreciated. I have a longtime friend who often is mistaken as my sister because of our similar features. When people ask about our relationship, I often overhear a response that saddens me: "Oh no, they are just friends." I want to scream, *"Just* friends!" She is the friend who stood by me when we adopted our baby. She is the one who encouraged me through graduate school. She is the one I called to help clean my house when relatives phoned to announce an imminent visit. The relationship goes beyond "just friends."

Lillian Rubin, in her book *Just Friends,* speaks of friendship as the neglected relationship many of us could not live without. I certainly cannot fathom how I would survive without my friends.

The search begins early in life for a friend to help shape and define us. Telling secrets, sharing emotional intensity, pranking and partying all come under the shelter provided by a true friend. I (Judy) remember the day my twelve-year-old brother, Don, proudly showed me the scar on his arm from a brotherhood initiation rite. He and four friends had sworn a solemn oath to lay down their lives for each other, to stand together through thick and thin. My cousin Shirley and I had another way of sealing friendship. We found secret places to whisper about everything that mattered to us. Revealing private thoughts about boys, teachers, parents and dreams ranked among the top joys of our childhood. In a pledge of loyalty, we promised to die before ever telling another soul what we disclosed to each other.

The inscription next to my sister's high-school yearbook picture sums it up: "A friend is someone who walks in . . . when everyone else walks out." Loyalty and commitment are the passwords of friendship.

Loving a Friend

If you want to be loved, learn to love. Our actions of love make us lovable. In the delightful children's book *The Little Prince* the fox describes in great detail how to love a friend.

Establishing ties takes time, the fox wisely counsels. A friend must be "tamed," a process too often neglected in our society. When you determine to tame your friend, you begin by sitting at a distance, waiting quietly. Looking at your friend out of the corner of your eye, you wait for the signal to take a small step closer. If that step is accepted, you take another, and another, until little by little you move close enough to connect. Following this model, the Little Prince learns how to tame the fox and establish ties.

Kay, Boni's friend, demonstrated that behavior. She kept showing up, allowing me to test her trustworthiness. I asked myself, *Can I trust her? Is she safe? Am I safe with her?* Despite my fear, the answers were always yes. Finally, when I had no more questions, Kay had one to ask me: "Are you going to risk being in this friendship or not?" Feeling fragile and easily hurt, I wanted to protect myself. But if I did not venture to risk, to meet her halfway, no real intimacy could take place. I could not have her love, companionship or support without responding. In taking that risk I have found a rare and precious relationship beyond my greatest anticipation.

Getting to Know You

A new friendship can be as exhilarating as a new romance. Having someone pay attention to us, pursue us and want to know us makes us feel important.

As we explained in chapter one, our own life journeys first crossed on Cyprus, a beautiful island in the Mediterranean Sea. We met at church and immediately drew close as we spoke. With lots of time available, and strongly desiring intimacy, we plunged in and shared from the depth of our being. We both have often wondered what allowed us to take such risks. Perhaps being in another culture caused us to feel particularly responsive when we found a kindred spirit from home. As we expressed ourselves with abandon, trust developed quickly. We believed God brought us together to bring needed healing in our lives.

With a willingness to be vulnerable we began to talk with each other from our hearts. We sat eye to eye and made a heart-to-heart connection. We began to discover how uniquely God viewed us and how special we were to each other. We felt known in a way we had never experienced before. Through asking and answering every imaginable question, we grappled with ourselves in fresh ways. We realized that becoming known would be healing.

Lifetime Friendship

A friendship goes through different phases during a lifetime. Normal movement throughout the years has a rhythm of invitation, renegotiation and renewal.

A new friendship is often experienced as idyllic, similar to the falling-in-love stage of romance, when everything in life seems brighter. You feel as though you have known this new companion for a lifetime. The soul-mate connection means you no longer feel alone.

You sense there is something extraordinary about this relationship. The newness brings exciting prospects of personal healing. Your most fundamental needs are being met as you nourish tender new growth. You give of yourself in vulnerable ways that nudge you into the fearful places. In asking and answering just the right questions, you gradually expose these hidden parts and let yourself be known. This gives you courage to find your lost self.

In this early phase when friends are dependent on each other, they can become overprotective. In Antoine de Saint-Exupéry's story, the Little Prince makes this mistake with the rose he loves so dearly. He decides to put the rose under a glass globe, because he fears it is too delicate for the real world. But he soon learns he must remove the protective cover so the rose can receive the elements it needs to thrive. The only way the rose can develop roots and thrive is to feel air, drink water, stretch toward the sun and extend into soil.

In the dependency stage of a friendship we need to be cautious.

Trying to protect new friends from the harsh elements of their world only undermines their growth. We prevent friends from developing personal resources when we fail to believe in their capacity to deal with their environment.

If intimacy is our goal, we must allow the relationship to be important. We give of ourselves, our time, our thoughts, our fears and our dreams. When these risks are taken, the relationship deepens and moves to a new stage.

Differentiation and Interdependence

The dependency of the initial interaction lessens when we move into the interdependent stage. As idealism gives way to practical realities, cozy togetherness gives way to more open space. We gain a new appreciation for differences, and new initiative is called forth from each of us. With ego boundaries intact, we can forge ahead with our unique voice. We can be realistic in the presence of each other. As Andrew Greeley says,

> We are both more relaxed and more sensitive, more confident and more vulnerable, more creative and more reflective, more energetic and more casual, more excited and more serene. It is as though when we come in contact with our friend we enter into a different environment where the air we breathe is more pure, the sounds we hear are sharper, the colors we see more dramatic, and the ideas we think quicker and more insightful. . . . The psychological environment is completely different, because now we are in a situation not only where we are free to be ourselves but where we have no choice. (Greeley 1971:110)

Mutual empowerment enables us to be ourselves and reach our personal potential. We challenge each other to reflect on the qualities of our friendships. We encourage rather than control. We shift back and forth with challenge and affirmation. Now we are ready for a deeper level of friendship, which comes through mutual covenant.

Responsible Forever

The fox advises the Little Prince on how to advance to the next stage, noting that we are "responsible forever" for those we tame. After we have risked becoming acquainted and allowed ourselves to know each other, the next step is to pledge ourselves forever. We make a covenant to love each other unconditionally. We promise responsible and intentional displays of love.

The two of us made this agreement as we prepared to go our separate paths in Cyprus. We knew we would greatly miss our times of togetherness, so we committed ourselves to maintain the friendship after our parting. We pledged ourselves to each other that day, exchanging gifts as a symbol of that covenant.

Not so long ago, another friend and I (Boni) made a similar pledge to each other. Neither of us had ever experienced the ritual of becoming a blood sister, and somehow in the fun and play of the day we determined to commit ourselves in this way as a symbol of friendship. So there we sat, middle-aged women pricking fingers, attempting to gather a drop of blood to bind ourselves as friends. We laughed and cried and sang the praises of long-term friendship. We knew an utmost seriousness undergirded our childlike ceremony.

When we pledge ourselves to dependability, we become more vulnerable. When a friend accepts the full range of who we are, we can call forth our exiled parts and let our rough edges rise to the surface. Being responsible means we are willing to learn the whole truth about each other. It means we are engaging with a real person, not a fantasy image. In faithful covenant love, we grow richer as we are healed from the center of our being. Our friend Kay Klein put it this way:

> I held the small stones
> for so long
> they left round body

prints in my palm,
numbing my hand
slowing the blood flow
making it hard
and harder to let go.

Here. This is for you.
It's only a small stone
but, see there?
That dark blur
like bruise
or wound, that's what
I most want you to see
and ignore
and want still to see more.

Trust

Intimacy is birthed out of trust. When trust is proven, friends risk much; when trust is broken, they risk little. The ultimate gauge of faithfulness is how we honor what has been entrusted to us. Trust is the shelter we need to produce self-understanding. Faithful friendship is a stance that promises:

I will give you me, I will not hold back, I will not hide, I will put myself at your service, will be willing to listen and to support, to run the risk of being hurt. I am yours to do with as you want, but my faith in you is so great that I know I have nothing to fear from you. (Greeley 1971:29)

Silence

Silence between friends is an intimate experience. Sitting together in tranquillity is a comfort. The quietness is not embarrassing, and there is no need to fill the space with words. In fact, talking would be an insult to the stillness of two people in communion. Basking in the warmth of the friendship is all that is needed; words would only undermine the mood.

In silence you can hear expressions you never heard before, feel emotions you never felt before. A friend recently asked if I (Boni) minded that she often says little. Truthfully I love that capacity in her. I greatly enjoy our ability to walk, sit or read together. It shows the depth of our connection. When she speaks, I listen, because I know she has something significant to say. Silence is more satisfying than any words could express when it is between intimate friends.

Play and Laughter

"Let's roll down the grassy slope!" Monica yelled to her friends Gaye and Jeannine. Their day together had been perfect. The bright blue sky and sunshine had lifted them into a spirit of frolicking and fun. They had a deep, supportive friendship.

Jeff and Jon threw snowballs and ran through snowy fields on their outing. They built a giant snow figure and laughed at their creative project at the end of the day. The rough-and-tumble frivolity brought out little-boy feelings in the men. They even made angels in the snow. Jeff and Jon had a feeling of camaraderie as they walked back to their cabin.

You can be known in wonderful ways through fun. When you lose yourself in the spontaneity of playfulness you are free to be yourself. Does your playful self emerge when you are with friends? My playful component loves to come out. She teases, jokes and laughs without being conscious of herself. She exudes an openness that is engaging and catching. In her whimsy she can draw others out of themselves. This side may not be found in a friendship that is too intense and serious. When pain is dominant, it stymies merriment and dampens the friendship. Friends who know how to play together know the healing power of laughter.

Separation and Loss

Separation and loss are one of the most difficult aspects of friendship. It is excruciatingly painful to lose a friend. Something inside us shrivels up and dies. We may doubt that anyone will be able to bring our inner self forth again.

Sometimes friendship loss is due to an unexpected geographical move. Though a separation does not automatically mean the death of a friendship, it usually takes a toll. Even though we can keep the friendship alive through letters, phone calls and visits, it rarely stays at the same level of intimacy.

You must work hard to fill the void that results from a geographical separation. It helps to talk honestly about how the separation will affect your relationship. When you get together again for a visit, be clear about expectations; otherwise disappointments are likely to occur. You will need to make concrete efforts to find ways to reconnect and reestablish ties.

Two couples had been close friends for many years when a job relocation suddenly put them two thousand miles apart. Although all four were emotionally distraught by the move, Dan and Jim did not make a great effort to stay connected afterward. Yet when visiting, the men easily resumed the intimacy they had enjoyed earlier. Sarah and Laura had a harder time being away from each other, and the separation had a more disruptive impact on their friendship. They worked hard to maintain their long-distance friendship by calling and writing, yet during visits it took them longer to establish their former level of familiarity. Each person must find individual methods to reestablish relationships after a separation.

When Friendships Go Awry

Sometimes a friendship dies from lack of care and nurture, or from irreconcilable conflicts. Sometimes one friend wants to stay close and the other decides to pull away. Whatever the reason, when a friendship goes wrong, sadness penetrates to the core of your being. The emptiness in your soul is great, for you have risked much and you have lost much.

How do you deal with a friendship that goes sour? Extreme disappointment usually causes us to retreat, but if the friendship is to be repaired you must first determine what went amiss. Friends must be able to identify the cause and then look together for a solution. The decision to recommit and start over is up to the two of you. However, if one party is unwilling to work on the relationship, the friendship may be irreparable. We then face the pain of knowing that our friendship is ending, as we will discuss later in this chapter.

Expectations and Boundaries

Sometimes unrealistic expectations become a problem between friends. One friend's demands can drive the other away. Greeley (1971:106) points out that availability must be rooted in respect for a friend's limitations. We must guard time for work and family obligations; of necessity this will limit our accessibility to friends. A friend may feel offended by our time constraints, wanting us to be more available. But we need to be able to resist the pressure to meet unending demands: we need to know how to set boundaries. A boundary—a border of personal integrity—needs to be permeable enough to let our friends in when appropriate, but defined enough to keep them out when necessary.

One way to look at keeping boundaries is to ask yourself if you can say no. Family therapist Carl Whitaker says if you cannot tell someone no, then you never really are able to say yes. Unless you believe you can *choose* whether to let a friend in, you will resent those who continually disregard your boundaries or intrude over them. You must believe you have the right to maintain a boundary. You need to be able to exercise your right when a friend asks more than you can give. You should not feel guilty or apologize for setting a boundary, but you will want to think through the ramifications of your boundary-making decision. If you and your friend do not have mutual respect for boundaries, you never will have mutual intimacy.

There may be repercussions when you tell a friend, "I'm sorry, I'd really like to be available to you during this difficult time, but I can't." Your friend will naturally respond with disappointment. But if you say yes only because you are afraid to say no, there will be negative repercussions of another kind. Resentment and resistance will be just as hurtful and disappointing.

When friends have the freedom to say no, they will have the freedom to say yes and really mean it.

Making Demands

The ability to decline a request does not mean that making demands in a friendship is inappropriate. Demands are inevitable and are definitely a part of any relationship worth its salt, as Andrew Greeley points out:

The very core of friendship, then, is the ability to make demands. He who knows how to make demands of a friend will have many friends and will be deeply loved; he who does not have enough self-confidence, enough trust in his instincts, enough willingness to risk all, to insistently demand response from his friends will, it is much to be feared, have no friends at all. (Greeley 1971:99)

Sometimes we need to be pushed to the edge so we can see ourselves in new ways. Sometimes it takes a jolt to wake us up so we can pay attention. Janette challenged her friend Diane to talk about the anger she had expressed toward her one day. Diane wanted to avoid the heat and retreat, but Janette insisted that they get to the root cause. This demand to get to the bottom of the problem proved to be a pivotal growth point for Diane. In the process of grappling with her angry emotions, they discovered the love underneath that made their connection even more solid. Diane became more confident in herself because she could embrace her anger rather than hide it as in the past. Janette had somehow tapped into the reservoir of anger she had felt as a little girl. Her impulse to cut and run would have taken her away from the pain, but when she could face this part of herself with her friend, she reached the core of the anger.

When Friendships Dissolve

Honest communication will help us survive most crises in our friendships, but sometimes friendships must end. Not every friendship has the capacity for healing. Some are destructive, and the best option is to end the relationship. No matter how painful the thought is, there are occasions when we are unable to transcend the barriers.

Most of us enter friendships with a storehouse of unmet childhood needs. Our childhood wounds cry out to be treated by someone who cares about us. We choose friends we hope can nurture and protect us, who will heal our hurts. We may be especially attracted to people who somehow resemble members of our original family. Unfinished business comes to the surface in unconscious ways in close friendships.

Jennifer was stunned to face the end of her friendship with Sandi. The relationship had started out so well. Inseparable in the beginning, they had learned much about each other in a short amount of time and gained valuable insights into themselves.

Close friendships had been an important part of Jennifer's life for as long as she could remember, but this relationship took on an intensity that had been difficult to pin down. The friendship seemed to be bigger than life. Jennifer appeared almost obsessed with working out issues exclusively with Sandi. Dependency and exclusiveness between them led to complaints from family and friends. Still, how could anything be wrong when Jennifer worked so hard to make everything right when they were together?

Then the relationship deteriorated. Jennifer found herself confused and disgusted at Sandi for various reasons. Her therapist helped her identify patterns that were obstructing growth in both friends. Jennifer grew angry when her therapist reminded her how similar this friendship struggle appeared to the previously reported struggle between her and her mother. She had longed to start over with her mother, but that opportunity had not come before her mother's untimely death.

Was Jennifer's therapist suggesting she had been using Sandi to work out unfinished issues with her mother? Was this why she had been so distraught by a friendship that had become too complicated to understand? That truth hit her where she hurt the most. Jennifer had fantasized that she could find a way to her mother. She wanted to be heard, to be understood, to be held, to be seen, to be soothed by the woman who gave birth to her. She had waited a long time to try to be wrapped in the protective arms of her mother. She had been shortchanged of that dream to gaze into her mother's eyes, to find forgiveness, to be connected, to let herself be known and to know her mother. It was too late for that now.

Then she met Sandi, a woman who actually looked a little like her mother and who had a similar personality. Would the friendship be one of healing or of pathology? Jennifer had subconsciously believed she could resolve the mother-daughter issues through the friendship. But Sandi became more demanding and judgmental—more like Jennifer's mother—and Jennifer fell into familiar destructive patterns.

When Jennifer started responding differently to Sandi after gaining insight from therapy, the relationship began to disintegrate. Jennifer stopped trying to please Sandi so much and stopped blaming her for disappointments. Surprisingly, a rage surfaced in Sandi. The healthier Jennifer became, the more reactive Sandi became. They reached an impasse. Jennifer had once asked how she could live without this friendship; now she did not believe she could exist *with* it.

Jennifer had to undergo some serious soul-searching. This difficult sorting process turned the relationship from bad to worse. The friendship ended with bitter, unresolved feelings. Thankfully, Jennifer continued to find her way through the turmoil with the help of her therapist. She settled her real mother-daughter issues rather than projecting them onto a friend. Jennifer established new friendships free of the dysfunctional qualities that had been part of her relationship with Sandi.

Healing Through Friendship

Healing comes when we are accepted and forgiven by a friend. Healing happens when we are empowered by a friend. Healing comes through disclosing ourselves and being heard and understood by a friend. Healing is the result of knowing another intimately and meeting one another's needs. Healing requires that we leave our comfort zone to enter into our friend's world. Healing demands that we remove our mask and show our inner being so we can be understood. Healing requires that we become real by honestly exposing our hurts and our joys.

God calls us to do the extraordinary so we can participate in the healing process of others. And when we do, our friends are part of the extraordinary healing that takes place in our lives. As I open myself to you, revealing my wounds and neediness, I face the reality that you cannot fix or fill the gaps in my life. This becomes my personal growing edge, for I must trust God to heal me. My friend will be at my side, to support, challenge and empower. We are stretched to the limit, to go beyond our customary inclinations, to walk the second mile with a friend. When we do, we grow. In opening myself to you, I stretch beyond my limitations. I become new.

Tina took a risk and told Steve she had been diagnosed with

multiple sclerosis. She feared living with the disease and wondered what the future held. Steve wanted to assure Tina that he would stand with her through the tough times. Frankly, he did not know if he could. As the youngest of three brothers, Steve had never really had to be there for anybody before. He had difficulty seeing himself in the bedrock role, and he shied away from giving the reassurance Tina needed. Yet as their friendship grew, Steve found the courage to reach out to Tina, to assume a role he never had tried before and to trust God for strength. The risk turned out to be profitable as Steve and Tina matured. God gave Steve the ability to be responsible to the friend he loved.

When we admit we are not supernatural, we touch each other with a common humanity that brings about healing. When we choose life, we choose change. When we decide to leave the old behind, we decide to leap ahead. When we determine to risk connections, we embrace healing. When we know our growth is a never-ending process, we make growth a lifelong process.

Our own friendship has lasted for more than twenty years. We have weathered separations and emotional storms in struggling how to maintain closeness over geographical barriers. We have found a renewed place of connection through our collaboration on this book. We had dreamed about the book during the first year of our friendship, for we believed we had something to say about how healing can come through friendship intimacy. A faithful friend is a vehicle of God's presence, a priceless gift.

Questions for Thought

1. What can you do to increase friendship intimacy in your life? Are you willing to take risks, establish ties, make commitments, make appropriate demands and empower your friends?

2. How do you go about establishing boundaries in your friendships? Examine your friendships. In which ones do you feel free to

say no? In which ones does yes feel like the only acceptable response?

3. Do you agree with the following statement by Greeley on making demands in friendship?

The very core of friendship, then, is the ability to make demands. He who knows how to make demands of a friend will have many friends and will be deeply loved; he who does not have enough self-confidence, enough trust in his instincts, enough willingness to risk all, to insistently demand response from his friends will, it is much to be feared, have no friends at all.

What is your experience with making and hearing demands from friends?

4. How does being overly protective prevent healing in your friendships?

For Your Growth

Think back to your earliest friendships. What was so special for you about that time? Make an effort to write a letter, send a card or make a phone call to one of your childhood friends.

Are there areas of unfinished business in your friendships that put strain on them? How can you discuss this with each other? What needs to be resolved?

Evaluate your ability to be a healing force in the lives of your friends. Which friends encourage your healing?

With a close friend, design and complete a ritual that signifies the commitment you each have to your friendship.

7

INTIMACY & HEALING
IN THERAPY

———

Two *ingredients generally thought to be a part of the therapy* process are self-disclosure and growth. So a book about intimacy and wholeness naturally should include a chapter on the healing potential in the client-therapist relationship. In many ways therapy is a deeply intimate experience. Most people tell their therapists things about themselves that no other human has ever heard. And, of course, the whole reason for being in therapy is to bring healing to painful areas of life.

The therapeutic relationship is incredibly personal. There are two people by themselves in a room, one listening intently as the other tells all. Thoughts and emotions are experienced in the safety of this special relationship. An intimate connection is made in this encounter. The therapist promises, "I'm here to listen to you and respond with utmost care and integrity," and the client opens up. As intimacy develops between them, the client shares a bit more, and the relationship gains significance. Soon client and therapist have established a tie that has enough substance to bring personal healing.

Intimacy often progresses when we take small risks with another, find that person to be trustworthy, then risk more of ourselves. Over time, as the therapist proves to be a reliable source of connection, the relationship develops into a strong bond. As the client returns again and again, trust is established and the connection becomes increasingly secure. The therapist is reliable to go through the deepest valley with us.

Going Through the Valley

I (Boni) had the good fortune of finding a therapist willing to risk the necessary intimacy for healing. Together we took a deep look into my heart to examine the pain there. The therapist then looked for an acceptable way to cradle that pain. It made all the difference in the world to have my hurt acknowledged and contained. She heard the emotion expressed and held it gently, unburdened. Without being critical herself, she could listen to the judgmental voices in my head and not side with them. She provided a protected place in my universe for me to look at my life differently. Surrounded not by voices of accusation and feelings of despair, but rather by words of healing and acceptance, I could freely sing a new song and dance a new dance reflective of the Spirit of God in me.

While therapy may not be necessary for everyone, for me it provided a place of intimacy essential to my growth. For many people, sufficient healing comes through intimate friendships, support groups, caring communities and other close relationships. But for others, those connections are not enough to contain the pain of brokenness. In that case, therapy provides both the safety and intimacy necessary for personal health.

The Therapist-Client Connection

One important way the therapist-client connection is different from ordinary relationships is its one-way self-disclosure. Clients pay for a setting that gives a regular time and place to specifically deal with their private lives. This intense, intimate time is for the client alone. Clients do not have to be concerned about the needs of a therapist, as they would about those of a spouse or friend. In fact, clients pay for the right to focus on themselves as part of a contract and need not feel guilty taking a therapist's undivided attention as a means toward healing.

Many clients enter the therapeutic relationship needing anonymity, not wanting to learn details about their therapist. As one client said to Boni, "I don't want to know anything about you, other than whether you think you can help me." This relieved her of any pressure of having to listen to my history. She did not need to worry about whether I had an argument at breakfast, how I was coping with my first child going off to college or whether I had PMS this week. She could be free to fully concentrate on her own concerns.

For others, being anonymous makes the therapy process more frightening. One of my clients could not respond to my questions without extracting more information from me first. She wrote the following note to me:

I cannot bear sharing my soul with someone I really don't know. I can't bear paying someone to listen to me. I can't bear the love I am feeling for you. I don't know how to function in this relationship. The loneliness I've discovered is overwhelming!

As you might guess, this client and the client who didn't want to know anything about me had different issues to deal with in therapy. Each client must work out a plan uniquely designed for her or his individual needs. One knew nothing about me from the beginning to the end of treatment except what applied to her situation. The other required more personal information about me: my marital status, a bit about my children, what hobbies I enjoyed. Yet even then we focused on her needs. My sharing had the purpose of providing a safe place for her. She needed to know enough about me, but not to the point of burdening her with my personal issues.

How Intimate Is Therapy?

Therapists have different preferences and capacities for how intimately they interact with clients. The stereotypical caricature of the aloof psychotherapist is one school of thought. But from our viewpoint, therapy is most effective when a client has an authentic encounter. We believe that emotional connection along with respectful definition of separateness between client and therapist is most conducive to the healing process. Therapists who have a clear sense of boundary can handle the baggage clients bring to therapy without being carried away emotionally. Clients need someone who can offer a perspective outside themselves and stand firm when processing information. However, we also believe clients need to experience a deep, emotional connection with their counselor in order to feel understood and loved. It is the job of the therapist to find the right balance of closeness and separation with each client. When boundaries are clear, the relationship has the greatest potential for intimacy.

We have defined intimacy as an intrapsychic process in which you come to know yourself through another. In therapy, self-disclosure lets the therapist understand a great deal more about the client. In hearing your story, a therapist strives to comprehend how circumstances look from your particular experience and perspective. The therapist asks questions and makes comments that help reflect you in a way that reveals fresh awareness and deeper self-knowledge. This is a demanding assignment, and no therapist is perfect. Yet the goal is for you to gain a better grasp of who you are through the connection. This interaction is emotionally charged for both, because both therapist and client are transformed by the intimacy between them. The therapist may be the only person with whom you can share the depth of your soul.

Fear of Being Known

The fear of entering therapy can be petrifying. A friend who started his therapy more than a year ago told us, "There is no greater fear I have ever felt than the day I set foot in my therapist's office. I would rather have faced a firing squad than to share my secrets with the stranger sitting across from me."

A female client who had no support system or friend with whom she could confide showed relief every time we met. Yet whenever she entered my office she agonized over what to tell me about herself. Being in therapy, while comforting, also created enormous anxiety.

Being a client requires great courage. Talking about the greatest pain in your life is not easy. Trusting someone you only see an hour a week in one context can be difficult. To be the vulnerable one in a relationship is tough. Fear connected with letting yourself be known is quite normal. The level of anxiety also is partially determined by the depth of your woundedness. Major surgery is more life-threatening than a minor operation, even though both involve considerable pain and agony.

We tell our clients up front that therapy will be painful. We warn them that circumstances probably will worsen before improving. We tell them therapy is similar to treating a festering wound. Just as a physician reopens a lesion to treat infection at the core, a therapist must dig deep to uncover embedded emotional wounds. Complete healing takes place from the inside out. Once we reach the middle, the pain is fierce. Medicine stings like blazes when it is applied to the most tender and vulnerable spots. Yet when you are hoping for a cure, even the worst pain is tolerable.

Therapists are trained to help reopen wounds at the source.

Treating the outer manifestation for cosmetic purposes is short-sighted because the festering continues, only to erupt in more disruptive ways later. Early on, some clients want to focus only on surface wounds because that is all they can handle. Only when you are secure enough in the therapeutic relationship will you go deep into inner pain toward healing. That is when therapy takes you to life-changing places.

Did I Miss Something?
Bonding, attachment and committed love are ingredients of intimacy. The appropriate time for this foundation to be laid is childhood. When children are loved, accepted and valued, they are capable of forming attachments as adults. However, if this emotional groundwork is stifled, the child ends up with relationship deficits—mistrust, inability to connect, defensiveness—later. In fact, the inability to make healthy connections in relationships is the primary reason people enter therapy.

For many, the therapy relationship takes on a parenting function. Everyone has some deprivation from childhood which needs healing. No parents are perfect, and no child ever receives everything needed. A therapist can help overcome childhood wounds. By having a new parent figure who responds to the hurts of your childhood experiences, you can eventually move beyond the point where development stopped. Rethinking the parenting process takes wisdom, kindness and patience. Therapists have a better opportunity to act as parents for the simple reason that they are not your *real* father or mother. Therapists are not perfect people, but the environment in which they practice provides the safety and stability needed to help you.

As a client you must show the pain of the child inside. For many, this distress is even more serious than they realize. Your adult self may be tempted to minimize or criticize such childish feelings. But if you are willing to become that young part again, the therapist can nurture your wounded child in an intensely intimate way. As the therapist hears the outbursts of you as a two-year-old toddler, you begin to see yourself through the eyes of a safe, loving parent rather than through the harsh, condemning eyes of childhood caretakers. This experience makes everything new. It allows you to share more freely, to explore the nightmares you have kept inside and to expose the secrets at the center of your being. As the therapist slowly uncovers painful childhood memories with unconditional acceptance, these parts mature so that you are no longer as fearful and angry.

When I (Boni) first met Tara, the timid young woman was full of anxiety. Leaving her house to do the normal errands required of a mother of three children usually would cause a panic attack. As we explored her childhood memories, she shared the messages her parents had planted in her head. Her father had repeatedly told her she could never do anything right. He watched her every move, criticizing and punishing what he deemed unacceptable behavior. "You are so stupid, Tara!" he would say. Or, "You embarrass me. I hate being seen with you." So Tara became self-conscious, fearful of acting stupid. In her mind she assumed cashiers at the grocery checkout line were criticizing her purchases. She could almost hear them thinking, *What kind of a mother would feed her family that? Look at the way she's dressed! What is wrong with that woman?* Her anxiety mounted until she had to flee to the refuge of her home.

Tara's mother taught her to accept her lot in life, that human beings can do nothing to change fate. If you are have trouble learning, too bad. If your father is angry and abusive, live with it. If you are a worrier, that's just the way it is. By modeling passivity, Tara's mother kept her stuck for years.

As Tara unwrapped these wounds she found understanding and comfort in therapy. She developed a relationship where someone believed in her, and her ability to change. She returned week after week to a parent who supported and affirmed her. As she began to trust that support, she could eliminate the misguided voices in her head and see herself as a child of God.

Can I Depend on You?

The client's strong dependence on the therapist/parent is inevitable in this kind of work. It may seem as though you cannot survive without your therapist. The child's sense of urgency and need for the newfound caregiver will be overwhelming at times. The client wonders, *Will she still be there? Did I disgust her? Will she leave me?* As with a baby-parent relationship, once you have bonded there are tremendous fears of being separated from your therapist/parent.

Mary became dependent on her therapist as she shared her painful childhood. Although one part believed that her therapist would not reject or abandon her, another more childlike part feared those reactions. She would work herself into such a panic she could not function. Mary then would break down and call her therapist, expecting an angry reaction because of the disturbance. Instead she received reassurance. As she repeatedly heard the therapist saying, "Yes, I am here," Mary's anxiety lessened. In time she learned to trust a loving caregiver in her own life.

Early dependence on your therapist is not only to be expected, it is sometimes necessary. Your therapist is ready to receive your feelings with deep regard and utmost care. Realizing that your dependence is temporary, your therapist will patiently wait as you grow into a more realistic and comfortable place of separateness and connection.

The therapist is human, however, and subject to failure. Finding that you are outgrowing your dependency should be a joyful experience. Sometimes that is not the case. Therapists with unresolved issues of their own may resist your independence and react to separation in a way that does not seem appropriate. Pay attention if you sense that this is happening. Talk with your therapist about it. Together you will be able to unravel the feelings you have and grow in the process.

Throughout this intense relationship a boundary must always be maintained. This boundary is the delicate place between intimate connection and respectful separation. As mentioned before, a client often becomes attached to his or her therapist because that individual is providing undivided attention for an hour or more each week. In such a close encounter a client can easily idealize a therapist. You may place your therapist on a pedestal and demand superhuman skills. Other relationships pale when compared to the level of intimacy you experience in your therapy session. You recognize the danger of dissatisfaction and disillusionment with your life outside therapy. The therapy relationship in many ways is an unreal one-sided and professional one. It's unrealistic to compare other interactions to those you have with your therapist. Your goal should be healthy growth through relating to your therapist and taking that development to relationships outside of therapy.

Nurturing Arms

We live in a society where people are virtually starved for nonsexual touching. To be stroked and soothed like a babe in arms can do more for some clients than years of cognitive sessions. Normally therapists reach clients through intimate eye contact, compassionate verbal responses and deeply felt utterances of understanding, and by offering a physical presence and posture that demonstrate deep caring. These are symbolic ways of holding clients in care. Such gestures never should be underestimated, for they are immensely helpful ways of "holding" clients.

Having clients learn to nurture themselves through imagery also is helpful. For example, we may ask the client to imagine herself as an adult holding a five-year-old child who had become lost in the woods. This assures the adult client that she has the capacity to nurture her inner child. We carefully set the stage by having the client be specific about the child's age, appearance, clothing, time of day when lost and so forth. These details put the client in close touch with her little girl so she can give her the comfort she needs in the imagery.

We also have learned that inviting Jesus to the scene can bring tremendous comfort. Judy had been working with Dave for several months when he first discussed sad and frightening memories of what happened when Jon, his overweight, mentally handicapped older brother, became angry. At age seven Dave had been terrified by this out-of-control behavior, yet he loved and wanted to help his brother. Dave thought returning to some of these childhood scenes in therapy sessions would be valuable.

Dave told about the day he came home from school and saw his brother being carted away to a mental institution. He had not been informed about the decision beforehand. Horrified, he had jumped on his bike and rode until he dropped from exhaustion in a deserted alleyway. He had hidden there for hours, depressed, angry and confused. Dave began to shake as he recounted that scene in his mind. I asked him to picture Jesus sitting by his side and to tell him how he felt about those experiences as a seven-year-old boy. Dave began to sob as he poured out his child heart. When Dave grew quiet, I asked him to let Jesus respond. Dave envisioned Jesus putting his protective arms around him and telling him how much he cared about what happened on that lonely, bewildering day. Dave allowed Jesus to soothe his heart and calm his spirit over an incident that had happened ten years earlier. He relived that childhood memory with a renewed sense of God's presence. Later, whenever he recalled the event, the powerful imagery of Jesus' support stayed with him. Beginning with that therapy session,

Dave's depressive tendencies lifted, and he had renewed energy for living.

Imagining your therapist or some other caring person nurturing you in a similar way also can be profitable. For some people, however, imagery is not useful. The therapist must decide how to nurture the child inside the adult. Gershen Kauffman, in *Shame: The Art of Caring,* affirms the client's need for physical, nonsexual touch. He is taking a risk, but it is one he is willing to make for ultimate healing. Whether to physically touch a client as part of therapy is a sensitive and sometimes controversial issue. An ethical therapist will certainly need to be aware of the implications of touch for you and proceed wisely. It is essential that the therapist continually discuss the meaning of touch with you. Holding your hand through a particularly difficult memory or putting an arm around your shoulder may help communicate caring.

Every therapist makes agonizing decisions about the ethical ramifications of physical touch. Some therapists have harmed clients tremendously through sexual touch. This is always an ethical violation and carries legal penalties in most states. The decision by a therapist to touch a client physically should be made with utmost care and under consultation with a professional colleague. Whatever the choice, a therapist must discuss how the need for nurturing is met outside therapy sessions as well. If the client has a good relationship with a spouse or a friend, this person may be the best one to provide nonsexual, caring touch. If the client is involved in a support group, members can provide affirming physical touch. A regular body massage from a trained specialist also can remedy the need for touch (see Berry 1993).

Stuck in a Rut

For many people, coming to grips with childhood feelings is only one part of the therapy process. Youthful patterns may still be operating and tough to shake. Ingrained habits are hard to break, and merely being aware of them probably will not cause you to stop. Women physically abused by males in their childhood become accustomed to being abused as an adult. Being beaten by a husband or other male figure does not even seem abnormal. The pattern of choosing violent men becomes a self-destructive behavior, even though the woman dislikes it.

A man dominated by his mother or other women during his youth faces the same problem. Likely he will marry a woman who controls him, even as he rails against the overbearing ways of his mother. In *Repeat After Me,* Claudia Black cites a poem that graphically describes the process:

Autobiography in Five Short Chapters
Portia Nelson

I
I walk down the street.
There is a deep hole in the sidewalk.
I fall in.
I am lost . . . I am helpless.
It isn't my fault.
It takes forever to find a way out.

II
I walk down the same street.
There is a deep hole in the sidewalk.
I pretend I don't see it.
I fall in again.
I can't believe I am in the same place,
but it isn't my fault.
It still takes a long time to get out.

III
I walk down the same street.
There is a deep hole in the sidewalk.
I see it is there.
I still fall in . . . it is a habit.
My eyes are open.
I know where I am.
It is my fault.
I get out immediately.

IV
I walk down the same street.
There is a deep hole in the sidewalk.
I walk around it.

V
I walk down another street.

To avoid the same pitfalls that have dragged us down before, we must purposely change our patterns. We must constantly remind ourselves of the hole in the sidewalk and choose another route. Until we recognize our destructive behaviors, we will never act to break out of them. We have become so familiar with the hole that we no longer see it. Often insight and efforts to try harder are not enough. We may know we are stuck but not know the way out. We are too close to the problem and need help to adjust. Developing intimacy with someone who walks down the street with us to warn us of the danger and point us in another direction may make the difference.

John describes his depression as a dark place with no reflection of light. He is blinded by the blackness and grasps for a hand to lead him. The intimate connecting touch of his therapist reassures him as he gropes along the way. Fearful of dropping off the edge or losing his way, he trusts his therapist to have the sixth sense needed to find the light at the end of the tunnel. As they approach, he relaxes, lets go of his grip and begins to make his way without needing to stay attached.

Christian therapists hold the hand of Another who equips us to do our work. Jesus is there for direction, protection and healing power. We walk through the pain and negative patterns of a person's life knowing that Jesus is with us as he promised. As the Holy Spirit leads, we find our way. We walk our client to a greener pasture, full of health and vitality.

You Believe in Me?

Therapists not only grant safety, unconditional love and acceptance but also challenge, engender hope and build strengths and potential. In this empowering process, action is as important as existing. In some ways the therapist acts as an adversary as well as an advocate. Clients come to therapy wanting simultaneously to change and to cling to old habits. They secretly fear that change will be too hard. Probing directly into these areas automatically disrupts the comfort zone. This battle can be especially intense in the early stages of therapy. The words of French writer Guillaume Apollinaire aptly describe this process:

Come to the edge.

No, we will fall.

Come to the edge.

No, we will fall.

They came to the edge.

He pushed them, and they flew. (quoted in Siegel 1986:204)

Through therapeutic intimacy clients can reveal, feel and embrace their pain. In the process they discover the healing that eventually launches them into solo flight. Even when you have a serious desire to fly, the edge is a scary place. There is a risk of plummeting to unknown depths. The reality that you might look foolish, crash or be injured in the process provokes caution and reluctance. The therapist is like the mother eagle who, at the appropriate time, pushes her young out of the nest so they will learn to fly. She gives her support by flying underneath, to catch them should they falter.

Many therapists believe healing occurs only through unconditional love and acceptance. While the intimacy of simply being together is a part of the healing, we also believe the therapist must be willing to be personally involved with the client in genuine, honest and sometimes confrontive ways.

I (Judy) vividly remember when one of my first clients told me bluntly that she needed more than a compassionate listener. The client sensed the inexperience of a new therapist and needed someone who would grapple more deeply with her emotions. She realized I did not challenge her as she needed to be challenged. She recognized unconditional love could not, by itself, heal her. I realized I still had a lot to learn as a therapist.

What About the Therapist?

Therapists are deeply affected by the emotional closeness they establish with clients. Intimacy is never totally one-sided, because personal matters affect us both. As we watch our clients struggle, our own feelings are stirred. We see the turmoil, we see the victories, we hear the agony of "exiled parts" (see chapter three), and our understanding of humanity changes. Our knowledge of God is challenged. We face ourselves in new ways. Our beliefs are on the line as we help in the journey toward health.

As Alice revealed the many parts of herself to me (Boni), one exiled part tugged at my heart in an unusual way. Alice was an artist, struggling with how to integrate her art into her life. She had many messages from her past that shunned her art as foolishness, not worthy of her time. As a result, she often felt guilty for using her artistic gifts.

As Alice disclosed this side of herself, I became aware of a gnawing feeling in my gut. I became conscious of my need to concentrate and force my directing self to take charge of the session. Later, as I discussed this case with a consultant, I pried open a neglected part of me which closely identified with Alice.

I had had similar feelings of guilt when taking time to focus on my creative side, which is music. Spending a relaxing afternoon playing my guitar would often leave me feeling guilty. I had not given permission for the creative side of me to function freely. I knew just what Alice was struggling with; I had exiled my creative self as well.

At the time I really did not want to examine this aspect of myself. Alice pushed on my growing edge. I could respond in any of several ways: I could retreat and become more clinical, I could deny the circumstances and mix up my issues and Alice's during her sessions, or I could responsibly work with a consultant so Alice's therapy would not be contaminated by my own dilemmas. Of course I had no choice: to help Alice, I had to deal with that area of my life. Along the way this proper course of action also spurred my personal growth.

If we are serious about our profession we find ourselves growing as therapists. Often clients will yell at us before understanding who really sparks their anger. We must appropriately handle rage that is misdirected at us. It is imperative that we hear these feelings and understand them, rather than add to the guilt and shame the client experienced in the past.

The intimate connection designed for a client's growth becomes a healing force in the therapist's life as well. This is true in all intimate relationships. We are changed as we partake in the healing of others.

Which Therapist?
How do you select the right therapist? Many states require therapists

to be licensed or certified, and that can be a helpful guide. Whether a therapist has been accepted by a professional organization indicates their training and experience. Personal referral by your physician, minister or friend usually is the best way to find a trustworthy therapist.

In your initial interview, inquire about the therapist's education, certification, experience, specialty and Christian commitment. Most of all, if the conversation is uncomfortable or you feel unsafe, trust your instincts. A therapist who works wonders for one person may be disastrous for another.

As your therapy progresses, growth will continue to be the major issue. Maintaining boundaries, sustaining the therapy contract, continuing confidentiality at all levels and ongoing competence are part of your therapist's responsibility. Violating these standards is inappropriate. If your therapist has infringed on your agreement, you may want to find another therapist.

There can be no intimacy without basic trust. Without intimacy there is no shared experience. If human intimacy leads to healing, it certainly needs to happen in the therapist-client relationship. Each matures through the demands placed on the other. Both emerge enriched and changed. The circular process of trust, shared experience and intimacy is the context for healing. And it is contagious, for experiencing intimacy in the therapeutic relationship leads us to intimacy in relationships with others and with God.

Being intimate, even with a therapist, can never be taken for granted. Intimacy must be cultivated, nurtured, questioned and pursued. In that close, protected environment, the Christian therapist has the honor of representing God in the priestly functions of confession, celebration, challenge and healing. We do not ask our clients to become what we want them to be, but who they determine God wants them to be. We cling to a dynamic living faith for the hope of our wholeness. Ultimately, healing comes as client and therapist listen together to the Holy Spirit for guidance.

Questions for Thought

1. Is there something you missed along the way that keeps you from intimacy with the significant people in your life? How might reparenting help?

2. What rut are you stuck in? Reread Portia Nelson's autobiographical poem. How can you reach the final "chapter"?

3. Have you ever thought visiting a therapist might be helpful? What has kept you from going? How does your fear of intimacy enter into this decision? What are you going to do about it? We encourage you to take the first step by looking in the phone book or calling someone who can recommend a competent therapist. Make an appointment for an initial session to discuss whether you could work together in a therapeutic relationship.

For Your Growth

If you had a particularly painful childhood, you may want to pay attention to your childlike parts. In a quiet, comfortable place, ask your loving Savior to nurture your hurting child. Allow yourself to be held close and gently stroked on your head. Let Jesus whisper words of comfort. Let your child talk to you, and listen with compassion. Tell your child you understand what he or she has had to endure. Grieve the sad losses of your childhood. Encourage your child with renewed hope about future healing and a restored vision for your life.

8

INTIMACY IN
SMALL GROUPS

Six *couples sat in a circle around a living room. They had been* meeting for several months with one mutual concern: parenting their teenagers. Their children made up most of the youth group in the small congregation. So they gathered, committed to praying for each other and their children. Now they listened as one couple shared about the heartbreak of their rebellious child. They thanked God for providing this place of support. They needed each other. They took the risks needed to be honest and vulnerable in asking for help.

In another group, seven women assembled for Bible study and prayer. Part of the structured group time involved intimate, confidential sharing of personal concerns. We encouraged each to carry out the changes that God had indicated as necessary. As one meeting drew to a close, an older woman said, "I would die without the support of this group! Everything in my life seems so hard right now, yet you stick with me and help me through it. I feel like I've grown so much, and it's because you've been here for me."

Half a dozen men attended a weekend conference exploring the characteristics needed to live as a Christian man in today's world. They cherished it as a rare opportunity to discuss with other men the pain and confusion they felt about their manhood. "I thought I was the only one who felt this way," one said. "I haven't been sure what a man is supposed to be like in this generation," another admitted. "I've been so sad about my inability to connect with my father, and now my son," confessed a third. These six men decided to meet for a weekly breakfast at a local restaurant to continue these discussions, a tradition that has continued now for more than three years. Each week they discuss topics as diverse as power, sex, fathering, spirituality, money, jealousy, marriage and work. Personal revelations have deepened their caring for one another, while conflicts and misunderstandings between them have challenged them to learn how to relate to each other in more meaningful ways as men. The small group has become a weekly highlight and a significant place of intimacy and growth.

In this chapter we will examine a variety of group settings and their potential for healing in your life. Some groups are made up of people who know each other well. These could include church members, neighbors or friends willing to meet together regularly in an ongoing group setting. Other gatherings, such as Alcoholics Anonymous and therapy groups, have anonymity as a basis. Group members do not know each other before joining, and identities often are kept private. These different kinds of settings appeal to different people. Both have the capacity for intimacy, and both can be healing.

Group Craze

Group intimacy. Is this a contradiction in terms? How can you share your innermost thoughts with a group and feel as though it is an intimate encounter? How can you trust and commit yourself to an entire group? How can confidentiality be guaranteed with so many members? How can you become intimate during one brief weekend retreat? How can you bare your soul to people you hardly know? These are relevant questions in light of what we have already covered about the importance of revealing yourself in the safety of an ongoing, trustworthy, confidential and committed relationship.

Self-disclosure in a group setting seems particularly risky. Many people have few qualms about being vulnerable to one other person but find sharing deep feelings with six or more terrifying. Yet during the group craze of the 1960s, strangers seemed relieved to share their buried secrets with each other in groups as large as sixty people. Amazingly, in such a large gathering many people could honestly and intimately express what they had held back. Lots of those who attended found the experience exhilarating because they connected with themselves in new ways. Unfortunately, group encounters inflicted wounds on others, as the following story illustrates.

A faculty couple, Duane and Janice Scott, traveled from Alabama to the West Coast in the late 1960s to be part of a sensitivity training group. They returned with great enthusiasm: the revelations had revolutionized their lives. They wanted to spread their joy to others, so they called a group of Christians together to explain the freeing experience. However, being naive, untrained in group dynamics and psychologically unsophisticated, they relied on gimmicks they had learned on the West Coast. Those who met under their teaching actually served as guinea pigs.

During one meeting the leaders asked Gerry, a group member, to go to each person in the group and say the first thing that popped into her mind. The shy Gerry had to muster a great deal of courage to do as the leaders asked. But hoping to free herself from inhibitions, she went around the circle and spoke frankly. She surprised herself by the words coming out of her mouth. "Sylvia, you talk too much. Wayne, you're so uptight in that white shirt and tie—why can't you ever let your hair down? Jennifer, I'm intimidated by you and all your psychological lingo. George, I'm really attracted to you." After she finished speaking in this blunt, spontaneous manner, she was not prepared for the aftermath of the exercise. She had offended just about everybody with her honest reflection. No one had been warned about the emotional reactions that would come to the surface. The episode took months to sort out. Gerry felt she had to apologize to everyone personally. She felt devastated by the experience and quit the group. The victim of untrained leaders, she had been rejected by all the other members. Not only were the subjects of Gerry's remarks stung by her comments, but they also felt guilty when she left.

Self-disclosure in itself does not bring instant intimacy. Flooding a group with spoken and nonverbal messages of emotional disclosure can be invasive, controlling and manipulative. There are no buttons to push or mechanical techniques to follow in order to make people open up in a healthy way.

Twelve-Step Groups

Twelve-step programs became the craze of the 1980s. Yet Alcoholics Anonymous started more than fifty years ago, when a Christian man established a program of mutual sharing and support as a key to staying sober. Since then the concept has helped thousands of recovering alcoholics and those consumed with many other addictive behaviors.

Part of the appeal and success of these groups lies in the nonhierarchical structure, plus the way unidentified participants are treated as equals. Leadership is shared. Common experiences with a similar problem permit a nonjudgmental atmosphere in which each member admits the dreaded secret aloud to others: "I am Sid and I am an alcoholic." The confession immediately sets the tone of vulnerability and honesty. Members admit they have no power over the substance and must depend on a Higher Power. Everyone is in the continual process of being healed, with no delusions that there will ever be a cure for the disease.

The group is committed to open and honest sharing. Participants not only encourage each other but confront each other for account-ability reasons. The con game is over for these experts in denial. Deceit is nearly impossible, because their peers know all about faking and hiding. Successes and failures are discussed. A balance is maintained: the one who has been sober for five months is praised, the one who gave in to temptation last week tells the truth. Some criticize aspects of the program, but no one can argue with its successes.

Kathy told us about the first time she attended a meeting for adult children of alcoholics. She sat nervously as others in the circle introduced themselves. Her anxiety level rose as her turn drew near. Her father had a drinking problem, but she had never admitted it as clearly and effortlessly as those in the room had done about their parents. Finally her turn came. "Hi, I'm Kathy. I'm an adult child of an alcoholic." The words spoken in a group setting had a powerful impact on her, and the tears rolled down her face. Stating the truth so starkly and seeing the supportive looks on faces around her gave Kathy courage to face areas of her life she had avoided. The group became a solid support for Kathy as she explored the impact of living with alcoholism.

Members do risk sharing openly in twelve-step groups. Everybody shares in vulnerable ways by expressing insecurities and wounded-ness. Those present do not judge you or flip out when you reveal your sin and pain. Many twelve-step programs provide the rare environment of open sharing without fear of incrimination.

Most people are eager to share themselves significantly when given the opportunity. The popularity of small groups today reflects our need to be heard, nurtured, accepted and loved by others in ways we are not experiencing in our significant relationships. Think of the number of people willing to share extremely intimate details of their lives on televison talk shows, blurting out details to a vast audience they have never seen before. When we are willing to tell perfect strangers our most private secrets, we may reach the false conclusion that intimacy is easily attainable. Sadly, many people find sharing their inner thoughts with strangers more soothing than sharing them with family members or close friends.

Therapy Groups

Therapy groups are where some find safety and expertise. These are groups with a professional leader who helps provide protection and guidance toward recovery. Intimacy cannot be manufactured in any group, but given suitable conditions, group members can open locked doors that had prevented deeper connections in the past. People usually are willing to open up in a secure climate of common brokenness and neediness. We reveal ourselves in new ways when we tell our stories aloud. And new listeners can help us discover ourselves in new ways.

I (Boni) am always a little apprehensive when I begin a new therapy group. The members seem to have so little in common initially. But as the weeks continue I realize people are so much alike in their inner needs. That is why groups work so well. As one member is sharing, others may be experiencing similar feelings and thoughts. The group can function as family.

I remember Carolyn in a therapy group who worked through her relationship with her grown daughter. She told us of her frustrations in interacting with her daughter. Often she would ask for our input. At one point another woman said that she felt smothered by the discussion. Having felt suffocated by her own mother's powerful personality, this woman was able to express something of what the first woman's daughter was probably feeling. As she expressed this, the mother saw a side of herself she had never considered before. Others drew from their own experiences and offered their ideas about the relationship. Of course, pronouncing a solution to someone else's problems is not always appropriate. But in some cases valuable feedback may be sought and received among group members.

Groups also can normalize our experiences or furnish a new perspective on our situation. A few months ago a woman in our group talked about how hard it was to relate to her dysfunctional brother. Another woman responded by expressing similar concerns about her own sibling. These women had established good rapport, as the group had been meeting for several months. Near the end of the session, the first woman exclaimed with glee, "I feel so much better. My brother is not nearly as bad as your brother!" They laughed, relieving the tension both felt, and thankful they each had gained a new perspective on the situation.

The group also can be a structured way of finding intimacy in relationships. For those who greatly fear closeness, the safety and boundaries of a group, especially one with a leader, can be a good starting point. You have a fairly good idea, in a safe environment, of how people perceive you. I remember Tom, a group member who once complained that his daughter would never express herself to him. "Why can't she just give her honest opinion on something? I wish she had the guts to just stand up for what she believes!" Later the man asked for feedback. Several in the group said his approach was too harsh, and they themselves were afraid of standing up to him, even though they were his peers. "You're kidding! I'm a mouse!" he replied. He did not come across as a mouse, but that was how he perceived himself until he heard from us. After he digested this new information, his relationship with his daughter improved.

Forming a Support Group

You can form your own caring group as a way to open up new pathways of growth. In beginning such a group, you must ensure safety and confidentiality. Nothing can hinder your quest for intimacy and growth more quickly than an undefined environment. As we already have illustrated, some settings are safe and some are not. Some people are safe and others are not. Be wise about establishing the place, the process and the people who will make up your particular group.

Sally and I (Judy) were both new members of a church. We found ourselves immediately drawn to each other as we talked about similar interests. She eagerly accepted an invitation to come by my house to get better acquainted. While sipping coffee together, we planned our own care group. We both wanted to share our lives consistently with a group of committed Christian women. We decided that the group should be limited to eight women so that everyone would have the opportunity to share each week. We established a meeting time of 8:30 to 10:30 a.m. Fridays, then asked a few women we knew to join. They had to agree to attend each week for at least a year.

The six of us who gathered for the first meeting could sense the excitement in the air. What a wonderful variety we had: a vibrant former missionary, a seminary professor, a feisty nurse from South Africa, a distinguished-looking retired accountant, a single mom of a preteen and a graduate student of Greek heritage. We each brought a unique flavor to our group. Our challenge was to learn how to find our connectedness.

On that first day we looked each other over, wondering how we could form a closely knit care group. The meticulous appearance of the reserved, distinguished-looking woman threatened some of us.

She looked as though she had it all together. One woman used lots of spiritual language. Another appeared quite intellectual and wanted to deal with theological issues. One expressed herself in earthy language. The two counselor types tended to take charge and psychologize. How could we blend into a group of intimates with all these differences? While challenging, our variety actually helped us jell. Our immediate task involved dealing with our differences, admitting our prejudices and accepting one another.

Ground Rules

We committed ourselves to arrive on time each week and to share ourselves honestly with one another. We do have some common ground. We all believe in a Creator God as our personal friend who is intimately involved in our healing journey. Jesus Christ, the wounded healer, offers us hope, salvation and grace. We look to the Holy Spirit for empowerment in all we are designed to be and to each other for working out the joy of our salvation.

Our pledge of confidentiality set the stage and tone of our togetherness. Nothing related during the meetings would be repeated outside the group, not even to spouses or best friends. We could share anything about ourselves, but not revelations others told us. We would rotate the leadership role each week. The assigned leader would take charge of the topic of discussion, make certain everyone had a chance to participate and end the meeting on time.

Growth for All

The group is still going on, and it has become our "cuddle group." Each week we greet each other with a warm embrace. We sometimes gather in a circle and join hands in prayer or give ourselves a group hug. We support and confront one another. We are committed to the personal growth of each member but respect each person's need and time frame to accomplish it her own way. We equip each other for our relational and work tasks and stay attuned to God's working in our lives. We find strength in our meeting as women who struggle with unique and common problems. No one takes control, and no one needs to play rescuer. We are equal and equally in need.

Accepting our differences requires grace. We make every effort to honestly express our reactions, to let each other know what we need and then respond. We listen to the hurts and difficulties we faced during the week and give input to increase understanding. We risk confrontation, knowing even negative stings give valuable self-knowledge. Because we are loved in this group, we can face the truths we tend to hide from ourselves. We challenge the stereotypes and biases that have kept us trapped in old practices; we examine our beliefs and expectations about the future. We are intent on personal growth and keeping ourselves and each other accountable for our goals. We delight in each other's dreams and hopes, doing what we can to bring them to fruition.

Growth and healing come from the new view we gain of ourselves. We are able to face blind spots and penetrate the thick skins that cover our true selves. The group is not flawless. We have failed each other. But we have forgiven and been forgiven, leading to the intimacy of healing.

What to Do Together

We often use imagery to help discover self-truths. I recall the time Karen had us create a sculpture of ourselves in our imagination. She directed us to take time to visualize the figure and carefully examine every color, shape and texture that came into view. After twenty minutes she asked us to share anything we desired about our sculpture. The varied symbolic meanings revealed much about us. Jane, the sophisticated woman in her fifties, described a beautiful Victorian porcelain figure complete with umbrella in hand. She discussed the fragile nature of her sculpture and how unblemished everything looked on the outside. She reported every detail of her exterior appearance with careful thought. But Jane went on to talk about the pain she felt over one of her adult children's struggle with a drug problem. Her façade of calm masked her inner fears. This exercise permitted us to look beyond the outside layer and tend to the deeper vulnerabilities.

Then, with a sparkle in her eye, Jane described one important element of her sculpture that had gone unnoticed. The woman's hair and dress had been windblown in a gentle but freeing way. We all recognized this wonderful side of Jane, for she had often surprised us with her fun-loving and spontaneous nature.

On another occasion a guided imagery involved a pottery shop where in our minds we each created a pot and filled it with whatever we wanted. Diane's pot had a crack down the side, representing a painful emotional scar in her life. But she stuffed it with a lush green plant indicating new growth and vitality. Nancy filled her oval-shaped pot with colorful fresh flowers, representing a celebration of completing graduate school and opening a therapy practice. Kate, the artist in the group, created a marvelous multicolored pot—but left it empty because she had been experiencing a temporary drought. As we listened to her struggle about important decisions, we understood the hollowness she felt.

Right-brain activities, such as drawing a tree, a scene from your childhood or the day you left home, provide rich fodder for group discussion. I will never forget the time we met three days after an earthquake registering 6.4 on the Richter scale had hit our area. We had been emotionally as well as physically shaken by the tremor, so verbalizing our experience provided relief. Elaine suggested we draw what we had experienced. My sketch showed a tiny figure under a doorway with ragged black and purple lines crashing down upon me. This being my first earthquake experience, I had felt sure the ceiling would crush me and I would die alone in my house. I relived the fearful emotions, recalling the desperate prayer I had uttered to God. Karen, the single parent, explained how she had no other adult present to comfort her. Kate had functioned well in the crisis with her children, but the drawing helped her unwind below-the-surface tension. After this time of common vulnerability we joined hands to pray for each other.

We have taken on creative projects such as sewing quilt patches and making a collage of our group. We have learned a lot simply by portraying a parent, sibling, spouse or child in our family and introducing ourselves as that person would introduce us. In that exercise, group members could ask questions of that family member about us. It helped us understand our perspective on these important people.

Sometimes we focus on a topic for a month or two, when each leader brings a related newspaper article, novel, movie review, book or idea. We have dealt with gender issues, spirituality, sexuality, women in the workplace and sexual harassment. The idea is not just to talk from our heads but to personalize by using our experiences as resources.

Laughter and Play
Periodically we go out for a night on the town, come together to watch a special video while a fire burns in a fireplace, or enjoy a barbecue with our spouses. One weekend we rented adjacent hotel rooms in Laguna Beach and spent our days sunning, riding ocean waves, watching sunsets, dining at swank restaurants and relaxing. We had no agenda except to enjoy ourselves. Karen brought huge bubble makers and soapy water for what turned out to be the highlight of the weekend as we giggled with delight blowing giant bubbles along the beach. Jane read a favorite children's story to us, Elaine led in construction of a sand castle, Judy oversaw relaxation imagery before we returned to our rooms, Diane administered a

backrub for everybody, and Kate gave each of us a seashell and a tape of Anne Morrow Lindbergh's *A Gift from the Sea* that she had recorded for our trip home. The weekend called forth the child in each of us.

A Time to Leave

When a member of the group decides it is time to leave, others will feel a loss that takes time to process. Pain accompanies any loss, and group loss is no exception. Emotional reactions such as anger, sadness and grief must be addressed. When the departure is premature or the loss process is cut short, the group tends to limp along or stagnate. This happened when Sue sent a note saying she no longer wanted to be part of the group. The letter came without warning. Remaining members sat silently in the living room and stared at each other in disbelief. Why did Sue decide to quit? Did I say or do something offensive? Was she mad at one of us or all of us? How come she sent a message rather than telling us in person? The questions kept piling up, but we uncovered no reason why she left without explanation. Guessing only added to the confusion.

Sue's departure rattled the rest of us for weeks. We resented the fact that we were taking so much group time to deal with Sue when she no longer belonged to the group. We felt rejected. We could not proceed until we could grieve the loss. So we asked Sue to come talk with us. We assured her we would not put her on the spot or lay any guilt trips on her. We simply needed some explanation. All of us were nervous that day, as Sue candidly told us her reason: she was unable to hear about our pain because her own pain was too great. She had decided personal therapy was needed. Sue explained that she had not intended to hurt us by the way she left the group. Ultimately we said farewell. The sadness remained, but the anger dissipated and we could let her go with our blessing.

The incident taught us a powerful lesson. Now we know we need at least a month's warning to process all the feelings that arise when someone decides to leave by choice or because of a geographical move. An event to mark that leaving helps the group handle it. With Karen we had several months to prepare before the actual emotional impact of her departure became a reality. On her final day with us, we conducted a ritual to help with the transition. Sitting on the floor in a circle, we each gave her a symbol to let her know how much she meant to us. Each member told Karen how she had impacted her life as we handed her the tokens. Kate presented a teardrop necklace to indicate how much she had appreciated Karen's ability to show deeply felt emotions. Elaine gave her a year's subscription to a magazine that suited her articulateness and sense of humor. Diane gave her sparkly earrings to symbolize a quality she valued in Karen that she hoped to develop in her own life. Karen received our affirmations, tears and hugs and had a chance to express her sentiments to each of us as well. We offered a prayer of dedication for her life as she moved to Tennessee.

The Group Renewed

When one member leaves, the group as a whole must decide who will be the replacement. We believe the decision must be unanimous so the new member can be wholeheartedly accepted by every member.

The group also determines the timing. Sometimes a certain member is at a juncture in her life when adding a new member would be too disruptive. Kate had our loyalty when she expressed hesitation about adding a new confidante. This request actually showed how she had grown, because Kate had tended to go along with the group norm even if she opposed it. She had been going through major changes in many areas of her life, and the Friday-morning group was her one constant at that moment. We honored her request and did not add a new member until Kate felt ready for the change. Trying to force a member on the group prematurely makes cohesiveness impossible. Kate felt reassured when we considered her welfare our priority.

When we are ready to add a new member, we suggest names of women we believe would be a good fit. We talk about personal traits and decide who would be good for us and how we would be good for them. When possible we invite two new people into the group at the same time. Together they can feel more comfortable breaking into a group with a long history.

We do not rush our decision. New members joining an old group are disruptive in both positive and negative ways. We can no longer tell inside jokes. We must update the new member about the details of our lives that everyone else knows. Adjustments must be made for the new member's ideas, requests and interactional style. Like any family's time of welcoming someone new, this is an important time of growth and change. The old group will never be the same. We must process the loss of the old in order to proceed with the gains of the new.

Prospective new members need to be given enough time to consider whether the group is right for them. We inform them that our invitation is unanimous, but we allow them a trial period, usually a month or two, to determine whether they want to accept. This gives the new member the privilege and responsibility of making a clear commitment. The group will experience a bit of instability until the new member decides. Then we hold an informal ceremony to officially greet the person as a permanent member.

Most new group members are somewhat intimidated to lead, so we allow them time to feel comfortable in this role by watching others. A signal that the newest member feels part of the group is when she challenges or questions some of the established customs. This is a good time to revamp what may need changing. We periodically make efforts to take a good look at ourselves so that we can be flexible to current needs. Our weekends away are excellent times to reflect on group goals and make plans to implement changes.

I have been in various women's care groups during the past two decades, and each is unique. Each has brought me to a new level of understanding myself and who God calls me to be.

Made to Order

You may structure your care group differently from ours. You may choose to be more inclusive if the group is made up of people from your church. You may decide to be more intentional, as in the examples at the beginning of this chapter. A group may be formed for couples or for Bible study, for instance. Some of the ideas presented here may be incorporated into your needs, while others may not fit. Our intent is to enlarge your vision of what groups can be in your life and to encourage you to use this as a means of growth.

Reaping the Benefits

A deepening intimacy is one of the greatest rewards of any small group. Ongoing relationships invite us to deal with our inevitable limitations, weaknesses and failures. Intimates keep us accountable. The small group is one trusted place that provides continuous growth and healing. Here we share joys and sorrows, victories and failures. Here is a place to be heard and supported regularly.

When one member is having a particularly difficult time, the resources of an entire small group can provide greater comfort than those of a spouse or a friend alone. You feel cared for when several friends follow up with phone calls, encouraging cards or gestures of kindnesses. Responsibility spread among many prevents us from being afraid of burdening one person with our load of concerns.

The regularity of the group establishes a continuity of deeply felt intimacy. My cuddle group gives me the insightful "aha!" knowledge that makes an important difference in my life. When I took a five-month sabbatical to write this book, heightened empowerment came through a ritual in my care group focusing on beginnings and closure. We each found a symbol in the home where we regularly meet to represent an expression of saying hello and goodby. Each person's symbol expressed a moment in her life's journey when an ending had been the gateway to new growth. It encouraged all of us to dream new dreams and to leave the old behind. My intimates knew the struggles of my past better than anyone else, so they could help me find hope in the future.

The focus on the future renewed my spirit. The anticipation of change and growth in the new year invigorated me. If you have no dreams you can never reach goals. We each lit a candle to symbolize a new beginning and lifted prayers for each person.

Intimacy has been an important part of every support group of which I have been a member. We know closeness, we have understanding through disclosure and challenge, we are free in our affection and appreciation for each other, we play and laugh, we can be angry and forgive. Our history of intimacy deepens our ability to know and be known.

In God's Time

A small group is one more way God can open you to knowing yourself in the presence of others. The group is another way God can deepen your understanding of who he created you to be and how he has called you to live. With the safety available in a protected setting, you can reveal the parts of you that feel stuck and search together for ways of finding freedom. Your group will support your growth, walk with you through pain and rejoice with you in victories. This level of intimacy is more extensive than what you might have with a close friend or spouse, but probably narrower than the intimacy you experience with your community. It may be less self-oriented than therapy and more self-focused than friendship.

You will be rewarded when you risk being part of a group whose members determine to know each other intimately in order to bring healing. When you choose to share yourself and to walk with others, you find real joy.

Questions for Thought

1. What is the difference between the encounter-group craze of thirty years ago and what is being suggested in this chapter?

2. What are the benefits in focus-oriented groups, such as twelve-step programs and marriage classes? How do these differ from care groups?

3. Did you like how the care group described in this chapter formed and functioned? How would you do it differently?

4. Think of a time when a small group helped you through a crisis. If you never have been in a small-group situation, what is preventing you from trying?

For Your Growth

Think about the kind of group you might need in your life right now. Would it be a group for couples, men, women, parents or prayer? Pick one person or couple you would like to have in such a group. Brainstorm what you need in a group to make it safe and to meet your particular needs. Consider the names of potential group members together. Approach these people with your idea. Let them know the specific day and time you want to meet so they will know immediately whether they can commit themselves to your group. When you have enough members, set the date and place to meet, and notify everyone involved.

During your first gathering, use the ideas from the care-group section to determine confidentiality, rules and goals. Make a commitment to meet together for at least six months, and decide how to share leadership.

9

HOPE OF HEALING IN COMMUNITY

As *I (Boni) walk into church on Sunday mornings, I always scan* the congregation in hopes of seeing Danielle. Catching her eye and then, inevitably, her hugs, makes my day. She is only three years old, but Danielle brings love and joy to all those she touches.

Danielle was born with a blocked small intestine. During her first few weeks of life, she underwent two major surgeries to open the blockage and to remove part of the intestine. But Danielle is a resilient little girl with a bright and cheerful spirit. Her big, wide eyes flash expression as she describes her latest trauma. "I fell through the window. I hurt my head. I have an owie right here. The doctor looked in my eyes. We don't fly like Peter Pan." On and on she goes. One of the youngest people in our church, Danielle brings inspiration and hope of God's grace. She gives and we receive her love. God uses her in our healing and us in hers.

A Place of Knowing

Our community of faith learned a lot about intimacy and healing from Danielle's responses to God during a frightening time in her young life. While surrounding Danielle and her family in prayer, our hearts joined in a love that had an impact on our entire community. In that togetherness we came to know each other in deeper ways. We became familiar with each other.

In spite of the struggles that any small community has working, worshiping and living together, there is one particular thing our body does well. Visitors to our church immediately observe an affinity among members. You notice how Josh affirms Mason. You see Karen give Judy a freshly baked apple pie. You find Darik praying with Dave. You hear Kay listening intently to Briana, a teenager in her youth group. People take time to find out what is happening in the lives of others. They are interested in knowing each other in this secure shelter.

Not long ago a visitor came to our church and sat in the back pew. Though she was attracted by what she saw, it took her a month to gather enough courage to become personally involved. One week she decided to attend the women's fellowship group. Even though most outsiders would have found the meeting too long and even boring, the obvious binding ties captivated the woman whose life had been solitary and disconnected from others. She soon plunged into the group, hoping to lighten the heavy loads of her defeated life. For the first time in years she shared her burdens and found relief from loneliness. Although she felt awkward at first, she gained the warmth of a caring community eager to know her.

Being known is a necessary part of being intimate, as we have shown already. Many of the relationships we have discussed will overlap in the church. We may have family, friends and support groups in the churches we attend and have intimate connections with a number of people in our congregation. But while these relationships will be the crux of our being known in our community, there is another kind of intimacy that is, in a sense, collective, in which the church body participates. It helps define us, extends the sense of where we belong and increases the areas where we give and receive care. These are experiences that require intimacy. If such opportunities are unavailable in our community, the church's ability to serve as a place of healing will be truncated.

A Body of Many Parts

We are bound together in love in the family of God. Our unique gifts are designed to serve one another. As 1 Corinthians 12 reminds us, each part is necessary for the healthy functioning of the whole. Each member contributes, whether the smallest baby or oldest senior citizen. The foot is no less important than the hand, the eye no more important than the ear. How would we walk with no feet or hear without ears? If all we had were noses, how could we hear? Rather than treat diversity as an annoyance, as we often do, we need to realize it is a blessing necessary for survival. We have been created to live in community, with hands drawing on the gifts of eyes and feet working together with legs. Our connection is vital if we want to function as a healthy body.

Likewise, when one member suffers, all feel pain. When one member is honored, all rejoice. The wounds of one handicap the whole, just as the healing of one brings blessing to everyone.

But aren't we all hurting? How can a body of wounded people help other wounded people? Shouldn't we be more concerned with healing ourselves?

A Healing Community

What makes a church a healing community? Of course honoring Jesus Christ is of primary importance. But given that we are in a biblical church that exalts our Savior, what distinguishes a healing group? Qualities such as safety, intimacy, grace, continuity, empowerment, love, acceptance and fellowship are a good beginning.

As we have stated before, connection is created and maintained through

☐ *covenant,* a commitment of unconditional love
☐ *grace,* a commitment of acceptance and forgiveness
☐ *empowerment,* a commitment of service and submission
☐ *intimacy,* a commitment of knowing and being known

After a summary of these principles we will show how each meshes with healing in community.

Commitment is more than speaking words; it is doing what I say I will do. Covenant love says we will be faithfully present and predictable to those in our community. We can be counted on not only to show up but to keep the pledges we make. We will be loving in our actions toward others and seek their good and their growth.

Grace is accepting a person without hesitation or reservation. We give others the benefit of the doubt and treat them with the same mercy we receive from Christ. We attempt to value the unique differences of others and praise God for how the variety of gifts broadens the community. Forgiveness is an essential aspect of grace. Differences tend to raise bristles even when we know that diversity is good for us. But grace conquers prejudices and allows us to embrace different people.

Empowerment is surrendering our self-centered goals and making the needs of others our priority. As we clear a path for others, we enhance their gifts and potential. As each member is nurtured and empowered, the whole community in turn becomes strong and effective.

Intimacy is stripping off our pretenses so we can see ourselves as we really are. By removing our protective cover we open ourselves to God and others. In our vulnerability and humanness as a community, we discover we are a people in need of healing. Through our fellowship of being loved, accepted, forgiven and empowered, we are being made whole.

A Committed Community

In this age of fragmented families, finding a church that has covenanted in community is a real blessing. To truly be in community is being family to each other. It is providing aunts and uncles for children who have none nearby. Establishing ties with believers provides us with others to share our joys—and our burdens.

A young family in our church recently had a tough decision to make about whether to move away because of a job offer. We prayed with them and agonized along with them to know the will of God. At last they decided to stay, and we rejoiced that God had kept them in our midst. Many of us knew they had made a real sacrifice by remaining in Seattle. They lost the opportunity to be with relatives more often, because the other job would have moved them closer to family.

In an attempt to live out a committed community, we threw a party for this family and gave them a present: a box of homemade coupons redeemable throughout the year. Josh, a teenager, would escort four-year-old Kevin to a movie. Kelsey would invite Danny to stay overnight. A married couple, Don and Boni, would babysit the children over a weekend. Megan would watch the kids anytime. Karen would give Jo a time away from the children every Tuesday. The box contained many other certificates as we demonstrated appreciation to God by loving this family as our family.

Not all people crave such familiarity. A family visited our church not long ago and appeared to enjoy the experience. They had been seeking a church home and said they liked the people and the preaching. But later they decided to look elsewhere because they wanted a place where no one would notice if they missed some services, where they did not have to feel responsible for others and did not have to be known in a personal way.

We have many ways of resisting commitment and thus intimacy. Saying we want to be involved, talking about commitment and thinking about intimacy does not make it happen. It takes energy and persistence to bring about a true sense of community.

A young man recently confronted one of our elders about some negative feelings he had about the church. He felt unaccepted and had a difficult time making friends. The elder devised a course of action to help the man feel more attached to the rest of the congregation. One part of the plan involved increasing his attendance. He rarely showed up two consecutive weeks, so the rest of the church did not know if they could count on him. But this seemed to be too much of a commitment for him; the young man realized he did not want to be party to a covenant that put expectations on him. Fellow members are now making a conscious effort to include him, but because of his sporadic attendance, he naturally will be left out of many activities.

A committed community is a force of love on our road to healing. Emmett Fox describes the power of our loving this way:

There is no difficulty that enough love will not conquer; no disease that enough love will not heal; no door that enough love will not open; no gulf that enough love will not bridge; no wall that enough love will not throw down; no sin that enough love will not redeem. . . . It makes no difference how deeply seated may be the trouble; how hopeless the outlook; how muddled the tangle; how great the mistake. A sufficient realization of love will dissolve it all. If only you could love enough you would be the happiest and most powerful being in the world. (quoted in Siegel 1986:205)

Covenanting in community is a commitment to stay with people through the hard times. When you are loved unconditionally, you have opportunity to grow. When you know your community will accept you and help you through difficulties, you have a place where you can risk dealing with the painful parts of your life. Only then will healing result.

A Grace Community

A broken people need healing that comes out of acceptance and forgiveness. This is how the apostle Paul described the model of a church that promotes healing:

> As God's chosen ones, holy and beloved, clothe yourselves with compassion, kindness, humility, meekness, and patience. Bear with one another and, if anyone has a complaint against another, forgive each other; just as the Lord has forgiven you, so you also must forgive. Above all, clothe yourselves with love, which binds everything together in perfect harmony. And let the peace of Christ rule in your hearts, to which indeed you were called in the one body. (Colossians 3:12-15)

A church where people are accepting, generous, tenderhearted and forgiving appeals to most of us. In a community that seeks to reconcile, members bear with one another and practice forgiveness.

But a church that promotes healing is both risky and rewarding. That kind of openness can be uncomfortable if you dread emotions or conflict. Jason wrote to his congregation to express what a difference his church family had made in turning his life around. He has allowed us to quote from his letter. After describing a childhood of sexual and physical abuse, neglect by an alcoholic mother and his own problems with substance abuse, his letter continues:

> Why am I telling you this horrible story? Because when I became a Christian many attitudes, feelings and beliefs were deeply ingrained because of the things that had happened to me. I was scum! I trusted no one. I did not trust any feelings, because even legitimate ones were instantly converted into anger. These things

did not go away because I was a Christian; in fact they seemed worse. I was hearing about my "heavenly Father," but to me a parent figure was someone who was not there, or if they were, it was to humiliate you and shame you, to torture you with the promise of good things only to capriciously take them away. A parent certainly did not take care of you and I learned early on it was best to keep your parents at arm's length. I could see no way of getting close to God.

These thoughts, feelings, sins, tore me apart and robbed me of my inheritance as a child of God. I was literally unable to contribute anything to the kingdom of God. No one seemed to care, or if they did, they didn't know what to do about me. Do Christians ever talk about anything that is real? Was I the only person who was this screwed up? These are the questions I asked, and asked myself. They talk sometimes, but always in the third person, not about themselves; the effect of that kind of talk is that "those people" have awful things in their lives, not "us." This is antithetical to the central theme of Scripture, grace. If God means for us to experience his grace, if we are commanded to do his work here on earth, if Jesus died to rid me of these chains, shouldn't that be expressed through people who would really want to know me and all that came with that, the horrible things, and love me nonetheless? People with intense shame aren't likely to make the first move, so why aren't we being encouraged to be the grace of God to others in this way? I have believed this from the early days of my conversion but eventually wrote it off as a pipe dream! Until I came to this community of believers, that is.

Now I'm worshiping with believers who are creating a safe environment for honest self-disclosure of awful secrets and besetting sins. This was the first time I ever told anyone about my history of abuse. What an incredible blessing to have someone hear that and still quite clearly love me! Over the ensuing months,

I continued to meet with persons from this community of faith and tell my story, acknowledge my utter reliance on God, confess my many sins in detail. And I heard these people pronounce many times God's unconditional acceptance of me (in spite of mounting evidence that I was "scum"). I repented and attempted to make amends as I could with those I had harmed (in some cases grievously). Breaking free was an incredible blessing and was significant in receiving God's healing of wounds inflicted on a defenseless little boy.

This healing has been extensive. My anger is largely gone, the impure thoughts are gone, and I have worked hard, with much success, at having a close relationship with my wife and kids. I am still tempted to periods of intense self-hatred and give in often, but God has been good even in this, as the intensity of these feelings has lessened considerably. I have, for the first time in my Christian walk, felt what it means to be involved in the life of a church. I have heard it said that "psycho-babblers" miss the mark by being self-centered in their approach to the Christian life. That's a crock. I owe much to those people who have listened to me, prayed with me often, challenged and confronted me in a loving way, and not been repelled by my screwiness. Many have been loving to me and encourage me in their commitment to a Christian life without masks.

It is easy to see why I have much for which to thank God. He showed me great kindness and mercy, indeed, "pulled me up out of the pit," through the group of believers I worship with. God has called me to encourage people to throw off the chains of deep emotional pain and the sins that often find a foothold in those weak places. I want to pray for that often, see him work in that way and give him praise for that.

What a wonderful blessing to have found such a healing community! It provides an environment where people can face the truth and receive the healing that points them in a new direction. Many other churches are able to offer a similar climate of healing.

A few years ago Judy's church conducted a reconciliation service that overflowed with healing and restoration. Dissension had caused wounds among members. We prepared ourselves through personal prayer and reflection prior to the service. When we came together that morning, the songs and Scriptures focused on confession and forgiveness. At a certain point in the service we had opportunity to make amends. One by one, members reached out to each other in gestures of forgiveness. We then received the sacred elements at the Lord's Table. As we came forward, the Communion servers washed our hands in a symbolic cleansing ceremony. This tearful, humbling experience revitalized our lives. Grace prevailed.

An Empowering Community

We have talked about empowering in a number of different contexts. Empowering our children, our spouses and our friends is part of being Christlike in relationships. But how does that work in the Christian community? How can we as the body of Christ empower others in a way that leads to their growth?

The hope of healing rests in the power of the Holy Spirit and is what moves us toward wholeness. Romans 15:13 tells us to "abound in hope by the power of the Holy Spirit." Through God's Spirit we have the hope of recovery from past pain and trauma. God's Spirit has the power to vanquish the past and bring us to a healthy future. An empowering community, then, inspires hope of healing through an affirming love.

Along with encouraging our brothers and sisters to hope and directing each other to the power of the Holy Spirit, there is more we can accomplish. We can grant them time ("I'll teach that class for you while you are in the middle of this"), permission ("Check that out, it may be good for you"), affirmation ("I know you are working hard on issues, and I think that takes courage"), encouragement ("I know you are dealing with hard things right now. I made dessert for you") and grace ("I know you didn't mean to hurt me. I understand what these days are like for you"). In such ways we empower fellow Christians, through patient love, to grapple with the difficulties of life and strive toward wholeness.

Chuck Swindoll tells a wonderful true story of grace and empowerment in *The Grace Awakening*. Two California whales swam north too early in 1988 and became trapped in Alaskan ice. Several compassionate Eskimos attempted to assist them by opening breathing holes in the ice, but the frigid temperatures thwarted their efforts. Other volunteers joined in the fight, and still more when the media reported the story. The National Guard brought in helicopters to smash the ice with five-ton concrete blocks. Russia sent equipment and workers to labor beside an American crew. In the end, the two governments spent $1.5 million to enable a couple of whales to breathe. Air holes drilled and smashed into the ice along the route gave them access to the open sea.

The saga provides an obvious analogy to our ability to empower each other to breathe, work, grow and heal. We are empowered in interaction when we actively invest ourselves in the lives of others in our community of faith. Sunday-school teachers, pastors and peers all take part in our faith development. They keep us on the cutting edge of growth and sanctification. Some will be mentors who equip us to take leadership roles. They recognize our talents and gifts and help us reach our potential. Some will support us through their loving ways and considerate comments. Some will challenge us through constructive confrontation. Our character is developed in an empowering community. Increased competence and confidence help us to find the healing and wholeness God intends.

God's way of empowering is radically redefined in the person of Jesus Christ. Jesus came in the smallness of a helpless baby and

chose humble servitude rather than strength and power. Henri
Nouwen spent time learning this truth while at L'Arche, a community of disabled persons:

> Handicapped people are very vulnerable. They cannot hide their
> weaknesses and are therefore easy victims of maltreatment and
> ridicule. . . . But this same vulnerability also allows them to bear
> ample fruit in the lives of those who receive them. They are
> grateful people. They know they are dependent on others and
> show this dependency every moment; but their smiles, embraces
> and kisses are offered as spontaneous expressions of thanks. They
> know that all is pure gift to be thankful for. They are people who
> need care. When they are locked up in custodial institutions and
> treated as nobodies, they withdraw and cannot bear fruit. They
> become overwhelmed by fears and close themselves to others. But
> when they are given a safe space, with truly caring people whom
> they can trust, they soon become generous givers who are willing
> to offer their whole hearts. Handicapped people help us see the
> great mystery of fecundity. They pull us out of our competitive,
> production-oriented lives and remind us that we too are handi-
> capped persons in need of love and care. They tell us in many ways
> that we too do not need to be afraid of our handicap, that we too
> can bear fruit as Jesus did when he offered his broken body to his
> Father. (Nouwen 1989:73-74)

Most people are reluctant to be vulnerable. We want to be impressive
and use every ounce of power we possess. We want to hide disabili-
ties, whatever form they take. We would rather be in control than
be in submission. It is almost unpatriotic to seek the gentle fruit of
the Spirit or to be a servant. Jesus challenged the long-standing
definition of greatness by modeling a revolutionary lifestyle.

An Intimate Community
How awesome to comprehend that we can know God personally. In

chapter two we saw how our soul longs for knowledge of God and how intimate relationship with the all-powerful, transcendent God is possible for believers. To think that the Holy Spirit communes with our spirit boggles our minds. The deep mysteries of God expressed through a human Messiah puzzle us. Yet this is precisely how Scripture characterizes our personal Creator God. We are invited into the inner sanctuary to know him intimately. In the process of knowing God we see ourselves in God's image more clearly.

One of the most complex teachings to grasp about the Christian life is that we are asked both to live for Christ and also to die with him. Romans 6:8 says, "If we have died with Christ, we believe that we will also live with him." Galatians 2:19-20 says, "I have been crucified with Christ; and it is no longer I who live, but it is Christ who lives in me." We are called to die to ourselves among fellow believers, living, working and worshiping together.

C. S. Lewis graphically illustrated what dying to self entails in *The Voyage of the Dawn Treader*, in which bossy, contrary Eustace Clarence Scrubb travels to Narnia with the four Pevensie children. On their voyage this selfish, spoiled bully loses his way and while sleeping is converted into a hideous dragon. To his horror he cannot rid himself of the ugly scales that weigh him down. He realizes that the greedy thoughts in his heart are responsible for his condition, so he cries for help in the deserted valley of his lostness. There the lion Aslan transforms his life. Listen to Eustace describe how Aslan strips him of the weighty scales:

> The very first tear he made was so deep that I thought it had gone right into my heart. And when he began pulling the skin off, it hurt worse than anything I've ever felt. The only thing that made me able to bear it was just the pleasure of feeling the stuff peel off.... He peeled the beastly stuff right off.... And there was I as smooth and soft as a peeled switch and smaller than I had been.

Then he caught hold of me—(I didn't like that much for I was very tender underneath) and threw me into the water. It smarted like anything but only for a moment. After that it became perfectly delicious and as soon as I started swimming and splashing I found that all the pain had gone. . . . And then I saw why. I'd turned into a boy again!

After a bit the lion took me out and dressed me . . . in new clothes. (Lewis 1952:96)

As with Eustace, the baggage that bogs us down can be peeled away. We too can feel the tender touch of Aslan's stripping away old flesh to expose the real person inside. We too can gaze into his eyes and sense the warmth of his breath as he speaks words of love. We too can be dressed in righteousness and become a new creature. In community, our transformation is reason for great rejoicing.

Ray Anderson refers to the church as a hospice because we can die to self there with dignity (Anderson 1986:157). In community we are upheld by others as we are being transformed. We are baptized in healing waters and proclaim a new life in Christ. It is where we receive forgiveness and restoration along our journey of healing. And when our wounds are especially painful, the community gives us hope that healing will follow.

Outrageous Pain

A young woman admits a secret she has denied for twelve years. No longer able to confine these thoughts to herself, she reveals her shrouded past in hopes of being set free. She trusts her community of believers and divulges that she was raped by her stepfather and two stepbrothers. The community responds with compassion for her and with rage over the grievous crimes against her. They uphold her while she expresses the pain and hurt within her troubled heart. They support her as she shares the humiliation and shame of her abuse.

They make no effort to hurry the process, nor do they impose an agenda regarding when and how God will bring healing to her soul. They pray with her, accept her and show patience through the process. They never minimize her anguish, nor do they prematurely offer advice. Unmasking her secret without condemnation is an enormous release. In this atmosphere of love and acceptance she begins to grasp the possibility of God's transforming, healing power.

Unhealthy Community

Although we all long to be in a community that promotes healing, we are not all fortunate enough to attend such a church. Criticism, slander, impatience and conformity are all too common in many parts of Christ's body. In those situations we do not feel safe.

Carol, a client, described her conversion and her initial years attending church. When she became a Christian she had great zeal for Jesus and hoped to become as Christlike as possible. She entered her new church family with all the eagerness of a child finding a treasure. She eagerly volunteered wherever a worker was needed.

She was ill-prepared for the criticism that awaited her. It began when she helped decorate for a church event. Remarks such as "We don't do it that way" left her feeling bad about herself without knowing why.

This type of criticism continued, but she persevered. After all, she told herself, only a few people had been so negative. Most were warm, friendly and glad that she contributed. But her eventual election to a church committee made matters worse. The fault-finding increased. For a pair of critics, especially, she could do nothing right. They only made recommendations for her own good, they said; otherwise how would she know "how things are done around here" anyway? Spiritual development lagged as she became caught up in petty carping about building maintenance and programs. Despair began to set in, and she wondered whether she could be a Christian.

*What if I really shared my struggles with these people? Will I ever
be good enough to contribute my way? Are these people safe?*

Unfortunately, certain people in that church were not safe. In this
environment she could not be healed by exposing her true feelings.
But she opted not to change churches. She had invested too much
of herself in that body to allow two detractors to cause her to leave.
Instead she found a supportive community within the community.
"Some people carry rocks, some carry flowers. I'm learning to stay
away from those who are likely to be hurtful," she says.

Fear is the culprit that keeps us from being known in our communities. Fear of being exposed, rejected, attacked, ignored or overwhelmed prevents us from telling our true story. Presenting the self
we think is acceptable is less of a risk. We are tempted to hide our true
selves when a congregation expects conformity. We soon master the
technique of impression management and present false fronts that
keep distance between others and ourselves. The church becomes a
hotbed of denial that hinders healing. When people accept only one
mold, those who do not conform are reprimanded or ignored.

In an insidious misdirection of God's plan, Satan has often convinced people that the church is the last place where people are
truthful enough to seek healing.

Just last week Karen's husband, Greg, accidentally cut his leg to
the bone with a circular saw. Hearing his agonizing screams, Karen
ran to the back yard and found him sprawled in the grass, both hands
clutching the bleeding wound. She quickly called 911. The paramed-
ics had to pry his hands apart to tend his wound. His instinct to
compress the wound was correct, for it halted the bleeding and kept
his arteries in place so that a surgeon could repair his leg.

This is how injured people behave when they feel unprotected in
church. Their automatic response is to cover their wounds and keep
themselves together until someone trustworthy shows up to help.
After being hurt once in church, people understandably shut down

to prevent a repeat violation. They grab so tight that prying their grip loose is impossible, unless a trusted friend anoints their wound so that they receive healing balm.

Frequently churches do not radiate healing potential. We want people who are already healed, not those who are in the recovery process. The wounded are too much trouble, not a good influence, not the true pillars of the church. We hope they move to another congregation so that we can concentrate on families that are ready to build the kingdom.

So many times we have had hurting people come to therapy disillusioned with Christ as a result of their experience with church members. They have shared their pain in community only to be told, "Forget it, that's over now, you are new in Christ, get on with it." Try as they might, they cannot be done with the matter at the moment. They hear the whispers: "If only their faith was greater, if only they would turn it over to God, if only they would read more, pray more, serve more, the pain surely would disappear." Yet the pain stays, the hurt remains unaddressed, and the believer feels powerless to change. In isolation the individual wonders, *Is God real?*

Our God walks through the valley of the shadow of death with us. We are expected to do the same. He is a God who binds up our wounds, heals the brokenhearted and carries our tears. We are called to do the same. There is no room in the kingdom of God for churches that do not tolerate, promote and encourage healing of the people God is saving every day. People who find salvation emerge from a broken society. They are damaged people. The community of faith, the dwelling place of God's Spirit, is our main hope for health.

God in Our Midst
As a healing, caring community of God's people, we can increase our intimacy with God and each other in many ways. Let's examine several possibilities.

Communion. The Lord's Supper is our invitation to meet God as a community. This is consecrated time to examine ourselves before God and in the presence of one another. It signifies our individual and corporate need for forgiveness, restitution and restoration. We repeatedly need to visit this place to be made whole. Nouwen describes this sacred and mysterious event:

> Take the Eucharist. A little bit of bread, not enough to take your hunger away. A little bit of wine, not enough to take your thirst away. A few readings, not enough to take your ignorance away. You stand there in a circle and you are poor people. And then you say, "The Lord is in our midst." Precisely when we discover our vulnerability in that circle, in the community of the faithful, we say, "Here is the Lord. This is the day that the Lord has made. He is among us." That is the fruit we enjoy when we join hands in mutual vulnerability. (Nouwen 1984:11)

In the breaking of the bread we acknowledge our hunger for the Bread of Life. In the drinking of the wine we indicate our thirst for the atoning blood of Christ. In our humanity we confess that we are a needy people who seek God's healing.

Prayer. To pray in community is to be vulnerable, for we stand before the omniscient God and in the presence of others stripped of our defenses. We admit our mistakes and submit ourselves to each other for intercessory prayers. The Holy One is in our midst as we pray for mutual healing (Matthew 18:20).

The atmosphere that provides the most courage to seek prayer for pains and hurts is detailed in 1 Peter 3:8: "Have unity of spirit, sympathy, love for one another, a tender heart, and a humble mind." Being of one mind and heart when we pray also opens the path to God in an intimate way. Falling to our knees to ask for mercy or offering praises in community is an intimate experience.

One of the most important ways we aid in the healing of each other is through prayers of faith. Those who are being healed of wounds themselves know the route to the Divine Healer:

Are any among you suffering? They should pray. Are any cheerful? They should sing songs of praise. Are any among you sick? They should call for the elders of the church and have them pray over them, anointing them with oil in the name of the Lord. The prayer of faith will save the sick, and the Lord will raise them up; and anyone who has committed sins will be forgiven. Therefore confess your sins to one another, and pray for one another, so that you may be healed. The prayer of the righteous is powerful and effective. (James 5:13-16)

When I (Judy) was fourteen, I developed a painful infection in my foot from a splinter that had been embedded there for years. One of my girlfriends asked if I had prayed for healing. I had to admit I had not even thought to pray about the situation. She gathered a group of friends around me to pray, even though I was a bit skeptical. But God used their faith to touch my life as I stood in the center of that group. The next morning when I awoke I found the infection oozing, indicating the onset of the recovery process. The small piece of wood worked its way out and became affixed to the bandage. This experience showed me, a new believer, that Jesus cared in a personal way. My friends had pointed me to the Healer, and my faith was strengthened.

God uses others to bring us hope of healing. There is a story about a famous preacher who delivered a powerful sermon about the love of God. As he greeted churchgoers at the front of the huge auditorium afterward, he felt a tug on his sleeve and found a little boy was trying mightily to get his attention. When the preacher acknowledged him, the boy boldly announced, "Pastor Joe, even though I know God loves me, I need someone that's got skin on 'em to love me!"

We do need someone in the flesh to uphold us when we are hurting and afraid. We need to be comforted by those who have been comforted, we need to be loved by those who have the capacity to love us, and we need to be encouraged by those who have hope.

Suffering. Too frequently we feel totally inadequate to bring hope to people who are feeling hopeless. Innumerable friends expressed their love and concern for us during the years our son Joel (Balswick) battled life-threatening chronic liver disease. Their comfort helped keep our hope alive in despairing times. The promise of God's presence is revealed through those who come alongside us in our deepest difficulties. The church, a gentle environment of healing, is a shelter that protects us from the ravaging storms of life.

Pain changes us. When God is involved, pain brings us to deeper places of faith and deeper places of knowing. As 2 Corinthians 1:3-4, 7 puts it, "Praise be to the God and Father of our Lord Jesus Christ, the Father of compassion and the God of all comfort, who comforts us in all our troubles, so that we can comfort those in any trouble with the comfort we ourselves have received from God. . . . Our hope for you is firm, because we know that just as you share in our sufferings, so also you share in our comfort" (NIV).

A few years ago a young man in our church was killed by a train. No one in our body was spared the agony of dealing with this death. Jim had related to every age group with his playful spirit and genuine helpfulness. We all loved this young man and feel the loss to this day.

Although we all felt the pain of Jim's death and we all needed help in dealing with grief, his family, of course, suffered the most. Often I (Boni) have heard his mother, Nancy, say, "If it wasn't for my sisters in this church, I would never get through this. You hold me up when I can't go on; you grieve with me and let me cry endlessly. You act as if you aren't sick of me."

How could we tire of Nancy? We look to her in admiration for carrying on the faith. Bearing the burdens of others is not optional for the body of Christ.

Joy. Raising voices to praise God together connects us at an intimate level. Praising the Lord in prayer, in song and in merriment brings us closer as a body.

We recall when we celebrated with a friend who finally quit smoking after we had prayed with him through many unsuccessful attempts. When he kicked the habit, the church celebrated by throwing a party in his honor.

We also fondly remember the morning Dave stood up in church to declare that he had committed his life to Christ. We had prayed for him for several years, some lovingly presenting gospel truths, others reaching out in practical ways when he endured a crisis with his teenage daughter. His wife had consistently shared her faith with him. We had a part in his decision and a part in the rejoicing during the worship service.

And there are celebrations when a child publicly professes Christ. Those are times for the community to exult. The whole body is blessed by a young person's decision for the Lord. Healing brings joy. Unified in gratitude, we sense a oneness in Christ.

Confession. Confession too is an act of intimacy. When we admit our sins, we expose our true identity. And after we reveal our secrets, we become accountable to others for continued victory.

Too often our past robs us of the richness of the present. But by acknowledging what is behind, we can embrace what lies ahead. If we do not heal our past we will not experience the blessing of the present.

In confession we weep together over our faults and shortcomings. In confession we drop our defenses and tell truths about ourselves. In confession we affirm that there is no more condemnation because of Christ Jesus. As we repent from our wrongdoings we can begin to move forward. We show remorse, ask for forgiveness, make restitution, settle our accounts and work toward restoration. Confession is a necessary step to healing.

An important role of the church is to offer the forgiveness of

Christ to those who confess. Many people find forgiveness by the Creator of the universe too much to comprehend. But fellow believers can and should joyfully remind each other of forgiveness in Christ.

Not long ago a young man who had attended our services stole some equipment from the church to support his drug habit. Later he confessed, and now he is paying twenty dollars a week from his meager salary to replace the stolen equipment. We rejoiced in his confession and the healing that began as a result. We also knew that holding him accountable was an important step in his healing process.

New Every Morning

When Jesus prayed for his disciples and for all his followers, he asked that all of us be unified so that the world would believe that he had been sent by God (John 17:21). When we demonstrate our oneness by living out our love for each other, people will believe that Jesus is who he declared himself to be.

The life worth living is the life that anticipates newness every morning. New beginnings and the hope of healing brighten our outlook. Intimacy in community shows the world a beautiful tapestry of the Christian life. God is the source of our hope and vision. Without Christ we will perish. If we cling to the truth we have the potential to be healed. God provides dreams to guide us into the promised land of healing and wholeness.

When Jesus healed a blind man (John 9), some Pharisees demanded to know whose sin had caused the man's blindness. They wanted to place blame on someone for the brokenness. But Jesus told them they had asked the wrong question. The correct question was how one finds healing.

We are broken people who need to confess, be healed and make peace with God as well as each other. We come to Jesus to be healed because we know he is the healer. And, as with the blind man by the pool of Siloam, Jesus takes his spit, makes mud out of the dirt and applies it to our eyes. He knows our wounds well, and in compassion he applies the touch that brings healing.

But he also asks us to participate in our healing. He sends us out to wash the mud from our eyes so we can see. Our action is an important, empowering part of the cure. We find the pool where others also are seeking Jesus' healing power. And we can apply the ointment to the wounds of others and then immerse ourselves in the healing water to be miraculously cleansed and healed.

Intimacy in community is a result of God's generous love, Christ's gracious forgiveness and the mighty indwelling of the Holy Spirit. We come together to love others as God has loved us, to offer Christ's forgiveness to others and to seek to empower fellow believers through the Holy Spirit as we ourselves are empowered. We are known as we never have been known before, for we are new creatures clothed in Christ's righteousness.

Questions for Thought

1. What are your particular fears about intimacy in community? Have you experienced broken trust in the past? How has that affected you?

2. Describe your most intimate moment with God's people. What did you experience emotionally? How might you draw on God and his church to meet some of your intimate needs?

3. What are some practical ways your community could improve communication, love, grace, empowerment and intimacy among members?

For Your Growth

Is there a secret sin you should confess to foster increased intimacy in your relationships? If you cannot say the sin out loud, try writing a letter to someone in your community expressing your sentiments.

Consider doing a group ritual in which you use the metaphor of the cleansing pool. Each member can apply a symbolic mud pack to another's eyes. Then go through a cleansing ceremony in which you take a wet cloth and gently wash the eyes, face and hands of others. Imagine Christ is in your midst, providing the strength to make you whole. Join hands and pray for one another.

For Further Reading

Anderson, Ray
  1986   *A Theology of Death and Dying.* Oxford: Basil Blackwell.
Berry, Carmen Renee
  1993   *Your Body Never Lies.* Berkeley, Calif.: PageMill.
Black, Claudia
  1985   *Repeat After Me.* Denver: MAC Publishing.
Breunlin, D. C., R. C. Schwartz and B. MacKune-Karrer
  1992   *Metaframeworks: Transcending the Models of Family
          Therapy.* San Francisco: Jossey-Bass.
Fox, Emmet
  1938   *The Sermon on the Mount.* New York: Harper & Row.
Greeley, Andrew
  1971   *The Friendship Game.* Garden City, N.Y.: Image Books.
Heim, Pamela
  1990   *Nurturing Intimacy with God.* Nashville: Thomas
          Nelson.
Kauffman, Gershen
  1985   *Shame: The Art of Caring.* Rochester, Vt.: Schenkman
          Books.
Lewis, C. S.
  1952   *The Voyage of the Dawn Treader.* Middlesex, U.K.: Pen-
          guin Books.

1963   *Letters to Malcolm: Chiefly on Prayer.* New York: Harcourt, Brace & World.

Lindbergh, Anne Morrow
1978   *A Gift from the Sea.* New York: Vintage Books.

Nouwen, Henri J. M.
1984   "Intimacy, Fecundity and Ecstasy." *Radix*, June, pp. 8-23.
1989   *Lifesigns: Intimacy, Fecundity and Ecstasy in Christian Perspective.* New York: Doubleday.

Oden, Thomas
1974   *Game Free: A Guide to the Meaning of Intimacy.* New York: Harper & Row.

Packer, J. I.
1993   *Knowing God.* Rev. ed. Downers Grove, Ill.: InterVarsity Press.

Rubin, Lillian
1985   *Just Friends.* New York: Harper & Row.

Rupp, Joyce
1988   *Praying Our Goodbyes.* Notre Dame, Ind.: Ave Maria Press.

Saint-Exupéry, Antoine de
1943   *The Little Prince.* New York: Harcourt, Brace & World.

Siegel, Bernie S.
1986   *Love, Medicine and Miracles.* New York: Harper & Row.

Sittser, Jerry
1985   *The Adventure.* Downers Grove, Ill.: InterVarsity Press.

Swindoll, Charles R.
1990   *The Grace Awakening.* Dallas: Word.

Whitaker, Carl A., and William M. Bumberry
1988   *Dancing with the Family.* New York: Brunner-Mazel.